CHRISTIAN
LOVE
IN RELIGIOUS
LIFE

CHRISTIAN
LOVE
IN RELIGIOUS
LIFE

SISTER MAUREEN O'KEEFE, S.S.N.D.

HENRY REGNERY CO. — *Chicago*

Nihil Obstat: Rt. Rev. Msgr. John A. McMahon
Censor Librorum

Imprimatur: Most Rev. Cletus F. O'Donnell, J.C.D.
Administrator, Archdiocese of Chicago

Date: July 16, 1965

with grateful love
to
my mother
a valiant woman of proven worth
from whom I learned
the first and best lessons of Christian love

PREFACE

RELIGIOUS LIFE can be a glorious and reward-
ing experience. Genuine sisters are Christian women in love
with Christ who have committed themselves to Him in a special way. Authentic conventual life, therefore, is a life of intensive Christian love in which the magnificence of human,
womanly love is ennobled, intensified, and purified in the
fruitfulness of consecrated virginity. Genuine sisters are genuine women who live the love of their vocations by relating
to God personally and completely and by loving people
warmly and maturely. Their apostolic influence is powerful
in promoting Christian love.

Christian women who do not love, on the other hand, are
a pathetic spectacle in any vocation. At best they may be efficient automatons, capable only of superficial responses to the
externals of life. When unloving women are in religious life,
however, they are even more of a tragedy. Besides being inadequate as human persons, they are deadening to the effectiveness of the apostolate.

Sisters, then, need to re-assess the total significance of religious life according to the dimensions of Christian love—the
essence of the Christian life. *The Convent in the Modern
World* described the richness of a traditional form of religious life for contemporary women in a contemporary world.

Christian Love in Religious Life continues with the specifics of Christian love as it can be lived practically and happily by sisters in our present society. It is hoped that *Christian Love in Religious Life* presents the religious life as an open avenue of satisfying and productive human fulfillment for real women!

June, 1965   *Sister Maureen, S.S.N.D.*

CONTENTS

CHRISTIAN COMMUNICATION

CONCLUSION

CHRISTIAN
LOVE
IN RELIGIOUS
LIFE

The Dynamics of Christian
Love in Religious Life

LOVE was officially proclaimed the chief Christian business when Christ declared: "Love the Lord with your whole heart, mind, soul, and strength; and besides, love your neighbor as yourself." (Luke 10:27)

Further, love was established as the trademark of applied Christianity when He said, "By this token all the world must know that you are my disciples—by cherishing love for one another." (John 13:35)

In the past, sisters have engaged in much sincere, but largely unproductive, theorizing about charity and religious life. Christian love in its practical dimensions, however, has not been sufficiently understood by them and so it has never been universally and effectively established as THE goal in religious life.

Holiness—true personality development which stems from a vital love-relationship with Christ and the radiation of this love to others—is not inevitable because a woman enters a convent. She must understand its implications and spare no effort to acquire it. A sister's task, then, is to become habitually competent in the art of Christian love. She must study the details of Christian love in action in religious life, and become a dynamic sister apostle—a real Christian woman—who loves God and people in a contemporary setting.

Primarily, a sister is a Christian woman who has chosen religious life as the means of fulfilling her Christian vocation

15

of loving God more than all others and her neighbor as much as herself. As the first step in devoting herself to the specifics of Christian love, the sister in the modern world must accept the responsibility of her development as a person and of sharing it profitably with others.

Self-perfection is not an end in itself, but makes a sister a better instrument in fulfilling the social aspects of Christian love. A sister apostle must be holy—it is not enough for her to be good. It is possible to be good; that is, to avoid sin, merely from fear. Only through a genuine love of God and people, however, can a sister become really holy.

Christ is the center of Christian life, and His love for His Father and for people is the model for Christian love. It is possible for a woman to fulfill her Christian obligation of loving God above all and people as herself either through the observance of the commandments in the married or the single lay state, or by assuming the added responsibilities of the counsels in religious life.

Learning to Love

If a sister—a human woman—is to be mature and intelligent in her choice of the way of the counsels, she must understand her nature as a woman, as well as the essential meaning of both human marriage and the religious life as alternate means of Christian perfection. She must not only be knowledgeable about the problems involved in living Christian love in the religious life, but also be informed of the advantages she may expect. She must be free in making her vocational choice and in living the love it implies. Any force or pressure, either of a physical or of a psychological nature, makes a mockery of religious life and reduces its redemptive value.

A sister must understand herself as a Christian woman. If an adult woman has had a normal childhood and adolescent development, she will have progressed through the successive stages of learning to love adequately as an adult. A child learns to love by being loved well by his parents and family or by those who take their place, and forms his fundamental ideas about himself and others from these experiences.

For the small child, demonstrative physical affection is identified with love, so that if you say "love your baby brother" to two-year old Susie, she touches her lips to his face and gives him a kiss. When she is asked how much she loves her daddy, she closes her little arms around his neck and gives him a big hug. In the event that she does not like someone, she refuses to give the affection. If Susie's mother speaks sternly to her as she slaps her little hands, Susie concludes that, at least for those few moments, her mother does not love her. On the other hand, when her mother shows obvious pleasure with her actions by giving her a kiss, Susie feels loved. So, for her, the expressions of affection are very closely related, if not completely identified, with love itself. This is all she can understand.

It is interesting to note how these reactions change as children grow and develop. A story will illustrate: a sister boarded a bus in a large city, and three little boys, ages 3, 5, and 8 were sitting in the front seats with their mother. In response to the sister's smile, the smallest boy who was very extraverted, walked toward the sister with his arms outstretched, and said with a big smile, "Oh, you are pretty. I like you. I want to give you a kiss." So, to the obvious delight of the child, the sister bent down and accepted the kiss. A little later, the Kindergarten child, with some hesitation, offered to show-and-discuss the toy helicopter he carried in his hands. Shortly afterwards, the eight-year old boy volunteered, with reserve from across the aisle, to describe his competence in riding the new bicycle he had just received for his birthday. Each of these children was demonstrating his affection for the sister, but the expressions of the love varied with their ages. It is obvious that the eight-year old boy would not have given the kiss as did his three-year old brother, because he now understands how to express his love in a more mature way.

The average young woman who enters the convent today has usually developed successfully through the most crucial years of adolescence. The influence of love has reasonably dominated her life. She has been loved and accepted affectionately by her family and teachers, and has effectively affiliated with her peer group. She has thereby come to understand in a practical way the meaning of self-acceptance, self-confidence, the security of being loved and of loving, and the rewards of belonging to a group and participating in purposeful corporate activity. Through these rewarding experiences, she has come to learn the meaning of loving and of being loved and, consequently, to understand better the Fatherhood of God, His love and concern for His children, and her need for loving dependence on Him.

Furthermore, she has learned the importance of status, ambition, and efficiency in modern society. She has become familiar with competition—strong and defeating on occasion—

yet, she is challenged by it. Rightly motivated, she is ready to do long-range planning and to sacrifice immediate satisfaction in working for a future goal which proves valuable to her and to her standards. She is determined in defining goals, sure in knowing what she wants, and shrewd in devising means of attaining it. A young woman strives for development of self and for economically and personally rewarding means of utilizing her talents. She is eager for self-improvement, and the healthy desire "to be somebody" makes her willing to accept sincere suggestions to that end. Basically, a modern young woman is honest—disarmingly so, at times. Even though at times she may involve herself in sham and superficiality of various kinds, she is not satisfied with these for long, and eventually seeks the substantial and genuine in life.

Generally, a young woman is eager for knowledge and truth, even though this inquiry is often hidden by a facade of lethargy which, at times, is not easy either to understand or to penetrate. She does not accept things at face value, but probes their pragmatic significance, asking herself, "What is it good for?," "Can it be used?," "What will I get out of it?" This questioning attitude is good, though possibly annoying at times, and can be directed to profitable channels.

From Kindergarten years—in some instances, even from the days of infancy—a young woman has been taught to develop her creativity and originality, and has been encouraged to exert initiative and to form habits of intelligent independence. She has been given opportunities for open-minded discussion and for cultivating and exploiting executive abilities. She has had to be serious in making decisions, since, in many instances, teen-agers of contemporary society are expected to assume responsibilities which, in other generations, were reserved for maturer years.

Her human desires to be accepted by others have been reasonably satisfied because she has been helped to examine what makes her really attractive and popular. As a result, she was experienced, in a normal way, individual admiration and group approval from others because of fine personal qualities. Undoubtedly, she has agonized periodically through the emotional involvement of crushes, infatuations, flirtations, and various sorts of hero worship. Ordinarily, she will have been emotionally attracted to boys, enjoyed social contacts with them, and probably even been "in love" romantically once or twice, at least for a month or so.

Somehow, through a healthy combination of all these normal adolescent experiences, she has discovered much about mature love. Through struggle for personal independence with its spasmodic rebellion against authority, the uncertainty of changeable moods, the unpredictability of developing emotions, the pain of adolescent indecision and fear, and the slavery to social fads and peer norms, she has learned who she really is as a woman.

The Womanly Personality

Through normal, satisfying contacts with men, principally in her family and school settings, she has been alerted to the fact that while the human needs of man and woman are essentially identical, they are fulfilled in ways peculiar to each sex. She has seen, for instance, that both man and woman need to love and to be loved as human beings, and that both can love genuinely and deeply. But, in general, a man shows his love differently than a woman. A man expresses his love for others mostly by doing and by making. A woman gives her love primarily by being and by serving. A man's love functions in a competitive world of creative and productive accomplishments, and a woman's in a unique structure of intense personalism and prolific submission. The young girl discovers that she has the particular qualities given to human beings by God, and gradually learns to know how she reacts as a woman to these needs and characteristics.

God blessed woman with special potential, in line with the purpose for which He created her: motherhood. Therefore, woman is equipped physically, spiritually, and emotionally with characteristics which make her efficient in motherhood. A woman does not, in fact *may not,* relinquish these characteristics when she becomes a Religious. Instead, as a Religious, she utilizes the same personal qualities which would have made her an excellent wife and mother, to become a wonderful sister. She agrees to develop them and to use them solely within the framework of her specific love-relationship with Christ in consecrated virginity of religious life. Likewise, the woman in marriage develops them also within the limits of her specific relationship with Christ through the conjugal chastity of married life.

It is a great privilege to be a woman! If a sister is to be a genuine Religious, she must be a real, feminine woman—and that means she will develop and use her womanly virtues and characteristics. The woman, whether she is in the convent or out of it, who is not a total woman, is unnatural and jars the sensibilities of those with whom she works. Further, the woman who develops masculine qualities is unreal and by her masculinity reduces her effectiveness as an agent of Christian love.

Woman, because she is a human being, was made by God to love and to be loved, and she must pursue that goal in any vocation she chooses if she intends to be truly a woman. When a woman learns the Christian art of giving and receiving love, she is a complete person. For a woman, love is a total experience in the sense that she is wholly involved emotionally. Her entire being is completely affected and influenced by it. Nothing takes the place of love in her life. If she does not love, she suffers a devastating emptiness, an emotional sterility which destroys her, and makes her less than human.

A woman needs to be loved for herself and to be needed because she is loved. It is not enough for her to be loved only because she is needed; she suspects this priority as expediency, so it does not satisfy her need to be loved intrinsically for her own worth. A woman needs affection and must be told in words and actions that she is loved. The noble woman also needs the security of knowing that she has the trust and loyalty of those she loves. She responds readily and warmly to the love she receives from others, and thrives on their devotion to her. Nothing can crush the spirit of a woman as completely as the infidelity or disloyalty of those she loves or of those from whom she has a right to expect love.

Woman is demonstrative in her love for others and often resorts to the use of superlatives in expressing it, simply because her love is strong and all-absorbing. In fact, it is limitless. A real woman never becomes weary of loving and of being loved. As she grows in the practice of love, she becomes love! The desire to share herself completely—to do for others, to give service—is an essential part of love for a woman. Therefore, woman is capable of loving every person. She tends readily to recognize the good in others and to be sensitively alert to their needs. So she can be generous enough to give her love and understanding warmly and individually to all persons, even though she may not feel a natural attraction to all of them.

The mature woman is self-confident. She was made to reign supreme as the queen of a man's heart as well as of his home, so she desires to belong to someone special through generous giving of herself. According to her human nature, she wants the assurance that she rates first in a particular person's affection. Therefore, she tends to want to reign in her domain. This puts an element of exclusiveness in a woman's love, perfectly proper to the one-to-one relationship between husband and wife in marriage, but which if not otherwise directed properly, may pose difficulties for a woman in group action of any kind.

This quality makes it difficult for women to live together in community and also for a woman to serve in a position of authority over other women. Her desire to be first also makes her competitive in doing things in a novel way. She strives for uniqueness in her love. She will be eager to be the most gracious hostess, to be the best dressed woman with the most charming personality, to be the most efficient and artistic housekeeper, to be the first to tell a bit of news, or possibly to invent some when there is a dearth of it! If the desire to be loved affectionately by someone who really counts in her life, is not fulfilled normally, she may seek it, and take it by force, if necessary, by possessing a person and smothering him psychologically by her domination. She may be jealous, seeing as a rival any person who threatens her affectional security or primacy with the one she loves. It is difficult for her to be objective in evaluating the reality of situations in which there is even a possibility of another person being preferred to her. This probably is the basic reason why it is sometimes difficult for a woman to hear others—particularly other women—praised. She feels that her security may be thus threatened. In self-defense, she may become critical of the person praised in the hope, that in "cutting her to size," she will maintain her coveted place in the affection of those she loves.

The natural and mutual emotional attraction between man and woman is very good. Woman is not self-sufficient; she was made by God to complement man, psychologically as well as physically. She depends on him for support, protection, and strength. She needs his understanding, encouragement, and objectivity. She looks to him for her completion in love and affection within the limits of the particular vocation she has chosen. In turn, he depends on her for a return of these fruits of Christian love which she gives with typical womanly tenderness and generosity.

This mutual attraction and sharing between man and woman is normal to human beings, and does not disappear with a religious vocation. Let it be noted that the vital cooperation between men and women is also necessary in accomplishing the apostolic work of the Church. If this heterosexual attraction is not cultivated and directed maturely, woman will "cling" helplessly to someone, refusing to make decisions or to use initiative in action. Or she may reduce the wholesome natural affinity between the sexes to the physical level, making it an orgy of illicit pleasure either in reality or in phantasy.

A woman needs to devote herself to people. In loving, she needs to deal with individualities—she cannot live and die for ideals or ideologies. A real woman, therefore, is generous, readily self-forgetful, so she can easily give more than is required in devoting herself to tasks which are difficult, time-consuming, and personally demanding—like bearing and rearing children, teaching children, nursing the ill, keeping house, or visiting the poor and the sick. To be happy a woman must be engaged with these or other practical concerns which give her opportunities to externalize her love in constructive ways.

The mothering qualities in a woman tend to make her attentive to and protective of others, especially of the young, weak, or suffering. When these qualities are not well-ordered, woman tends to be possessive and even to domineer others, or to be over-directive in her concern for them. She has great capacity for detail—the nobility of attention to the fine points of life—which is so essential in giving thoughtful love and consideration to others. Taken out of bounds, however, this trait may lead to petty and picayune attention to nonessentials.

A genuine woman has strength of purpose and is dependable and steadfast. She is courageous and enduring in her love. A woman who loves is long-suffering—she can wait patiently and silently when necessary. She has power to bear pain without complaint over a long period of time. Her powers of endurance and her frustration tolerance are strong. The woman who really loves is ready to excuse mistakes and to help people profit by them. She can be undaunted in her loyalty to those she loves, and can forgive without qualification because she is able to love purely and unselfishly. Since she is sympathetic, she can easily concentrate her attention on others and identify herself with their sufferings and pain, as well as their joys. She need not have initial emotional ties to those with whom she sympathizes, but can love other human beings just because they need her patience in trusting and understanding them.

A woman can give her love to others even when it is unrequited by them, provided she is simultaneously loved well by the people who count in her life. She understands that people learn to love by being loved wisely and warmly. She prays for them, overlooks their shortcomings, and spares them hurt or heartache whenever she can. She has the patience to wait until her love fructifies in the hearts of those who do not love.

Woman senses things because she is strongly motivated by her feelings. She often thinks with her heart and, on occasion, may follow a conscience based on emotion rather than reason. She has a lively imagination and uses it often in relating intimately and personally to people and to her surroundings. For this reason, she finds it difficult to develop objectivity in evaluating herself, people, and circumstances with which she is concerned.

The mature woman who loves is tender and warm in her

compassion. She can listen with her heart as well as with her ears. She understands things that are not said, and says things without moving her lips. Her thoughtfulness anticipates the needs of others, and finds expression in consideration for them. She is selfless in her love and has a keen sensitivity to the feelings of others. Her sympathy is often intensified in direct proportion to the degree to which she herself has experiential knowledge of circumstances.

A woman who loves must suffer. Something in a woman remains undeveloped when she has not suffered well. Woman has great capacity for suffering, and because she is natively patient, devoted, and faithful, she becomes more fulfilled, more developed, more Christ-like when her potential has been tapped by suffering, intelligently accepted. Suffering is identified in a very intimate, perhaps mystical, way with love in the life of a woman.

The woman who loves has a certain intensity about the way she approaches life, which makes her warm, energetic, enthusiastic, sincere, optimistic, and interested. She is alive and alert! She is joyous! Joy, the immediate emotional delight in anticipating or acquiring good in specific instances, is an integral prerogative of Christian love. Happiness is an enduring state of joy which, for a woman, is synonymous with love. It is a relatively permanent contentment and wellbeing which emanates from real and continual giving of self. It is the imperturable peace flowing from devoted compliance to the many-faceted plenitude of Christian love.

And when her days of little-girl make-believe are over, a young woman dreams many wonderful dreams of a future that is real. Undoubtedly, at some time or other, because she is a woman, her phantasy turns to the ideal man whom she will someday marry. It is good that she visualizes definitely the qualifications of this person with whom she desires to share her life in marriage. The vision, of course, is ideal. He will love her warmly and more than all others because he respects and treasures her for her own sake. He will be intelligent, interested in ideas, and capable of aesthetic appreciations comparable to hers. He will be a strong man, pure and unselfish, kind and honest, considerate and generous, with sound values and attitudes. He will be a good provider, steady at his work. She will give herself to him totally —loving him completely. They will be in love in a wonderful, one-to-one intimate and affectionate relationship which they will bless by pledging their mutual fidelity in a vow of marriage. Together, they will become holy—really loving God and people—through the intensification and extension of their love for each other. And then to make the dream complete, some day their love will fructify—and she will become a mother. Motherhood is the completion of love for a woman in a happy marriage. It is, for her, the culmination of earthly joy and satisfaction because her children are the fruit of the mutual love she shares with her husband.

All her childhood and adolescent experiences—idealistic and realistic—help a young lady to understand herself as a woman. They also provide opportunities for her to develop discernment and discrimination which make her mature in her judgments, reactions, and abilities. Through realistic experiences, the gilt of her dream wears off, but the genuine meaning and beauty of marriage become more of a reality for her. When a woman decides to fulfill her Christian obligation of loving God and people through marriage, she chooses a husband—a man—another human being like herself with whom she shares a mutual love-relationship and to whom she makes the perfect gift of herself. Her husband, then, becomes a mediator between herself and Christ, and she becomes one for him in the same way. She has certain joys, privileges, obligations, and adjustments in accepting this Christian commitment of love in marriage. The woman who chooses marriage must understand what it means for her as a Christian, if it is to become a truly ennobling means of sanctification for her, her husband, and their children. This is the woman in love who thinks only of what she can give. All circumstances in her life are interpreted in the light of her love.

Religious Vocation

In looking for the ideal man with whom to share her life, a young woman may come to know Christ and to discover that He has the qualities for which she is searching in a husband. Therefore, she understands and accepts His invitation to love Him directly in religious life as a sister without the mediation of a husband in marriage. Thus, she chooses a person—Christ. So in deciding to practice her Christian commitment of love by following a religious vocation, she—this total human woman—now in love with Christ, decides to share her life with Him and seals her love for Him through a vow of consecrated virginal chastity in religious life. She becomes a sister and thus makes a complete gift of herself to Christ. This unique love-relationship, also, is real, but it

is based on faith. This does not, in any way, deny fulfillment to her as a woman, but it requires a re-directing of
some of woman's most basic natural qualities, needs, and
desires. If loving in religious life is to be an efficacious and
enriching Christian activity for a sister, she must maintain
and develop her complete humanness, and know and understand the joys, privileges, obligations, and adjustments which
are involved in this gift of herself to Christ.

The vow of chastity taken by a religious woman is a con-
secration of her complete being through her personal love
for and devotion to Christ. Rightfully, then, the vow of chastity—the vow of love—is for her as a woman the most significant of the vows because it gives meaning and purpose not
only to obedience and poverty, but to all else in her life. It
is her love-pact with Christ and is positive in all its implications. It gives her a right to love and to be loved by Him in
a specific way, and to love all other people freely, intensely,
and completely for their own sakes as He loves them. Her
love for Him and for His brothers and sisters are so identified
that they are functionally inseparable.

If a sister really loves God, she must also love people, and
only when she genuinely loves people is she able to relate
significantly to Him. She can never love God more by loving
people less. In fact, while her love for God always should be
appreciatively highest, ordinarily, her love for people will be
affectionately greater. The equation of Christian love is sym-
metrically balanced—love of God equals love of people and
vice versa! Further, love gives her strength to oppose the foes
of love—hatred, prejudice, antagonism, and coldness—which
defy the very purpose for which human beings were created.

In this way she realizes the fullness of spiritual motherhood, even though, with complete knowledge, freedom, and appreciation, she foregoes the privilege of marriage and physical motherhood—for a woman—the supreme proof of her love for Christ.

The scope of her love is, in one sense, unbounded—Christian love and all its concerns are her business. Yet, it has a specificity of its own, since her practice of Christian love must be structured within the prescriptions of religious life. In appraising her religious vocation, a sister does not stress the element of sacrifice—the "give up" idea—as the center of her life. Viewed in the light of love, a sister did not give up so much in becoming a Religious. Surely a sister makes sacrifices, many of them identical with, many different from, those of lay women. Who is to say, however, that a sister in fulfilling her Christian commitment in religious life makes more or greater personal sacrifices than lay women living their vocations as Christians in marriage or in the single lay state? A sister knows that vital, practical Christian love is the dynamic element in religious life, and that kindness, sacrifice, labor, prayer, penance, joy, failure, professional preparation, and all else take on meaning only when examined in this perspective. Love gives vision to see over and beyond the pettiness of life and to expand thoughts, hopes, and deeds to broader limits. A sister is a woman in love—in love with Christ—and a woman in love, thinks only of all she can give, because real love—giving of self—is everything to a genuine woman.

There is no need for martyr complexes or delusions of heroism which deify generosity and detachment in religious life. Love is the life of a real sister, so she does not measure her giving in terms of sacrifice or equate her freedom to love universally with personal deprivation. She does not feel cheated in any way. She sees detachment for what it is—the liberation from mundane and selfish concerns so she, a sister apostle, has time and freedom to love. This is the romance of religious life—the complete fulfillment of womanhood for a sister—a flesh-and-blood, sweat-and-tears, joy-and-peace business of loving Christ as a person and people for their own sakes in and through Him. This is the process of genuine holiness—an awesome experience.

Love clarifies the implications of the other two vows taken by a sister. Consecrated poverty for a religious woman is not economic security or a holy right to the abundance of life, nor is it the poverty of destitution. Rather, it signifies an ability to love which enables a sister to use the gifts of God with maximum effectiveness in the apostolate. This means that she accepts humbly from God what she is, the circumstances under which she lives and works, and the companions He chooses for her. It gives her the magnanimity of intelligent renunciation, and brings forth in her a nobility in sacrificing personal convenience for the common good when necessary. Thus she is happy in perceiving the good in life and in sharing it with others.

Religious obedience is not the right to shun adult responsibility in immature dependence and selfishness. Rather, love makes it an opportunity to develop personal potential and individuality and to exert diligent efforts to form habits of rational living. It is readiness to serve Christ selflessly in His Kingdom. True religious obedience, informed by love, implies the mature cooperation of real women under the direction of legally constituted authority. In this genuine approach to sanctity, a sister appreciates her dependence on God, understands that usually He manifests His designs for her through creatures, and accepts, by faith, the truth that He providentially supervises every phase of her life.

A sister knows that in giving herself to Christ as a Religious, she has not done Him a favor, but, on the contrary, has been favored by Him as the recipient of His special blessings and compensations. These blessings include the peace and joy of loving and being loved by Christ through consecrated commitment, the opportunity for personal Christian fulfillment, the support of love in conventual family life, the satisfactions of giving unselfishly to others in a social service apostolate, and, finally, the promise of an eternal reward of perfect love!

A sister will realize, however, that it will often be painful to human nature realistically to live this life of love in faith, just as, often, it is painful to lay Christians to perform their obligations in either the married or the single state. All Christians must live a life of faith. Christian love sets the limits and provides the motivation for mature living in every vocation, so the pain and frustrations involved in living a life of love are common problems for all Christians. The essentials and principles of love are identical for all Christians— only the details of practice differ according to the nature of the particular vocation.

A sister must really know Christ as a person if she is to love Him as she ought. This is the crucial factor for each sister and gives meaning to her life as a Religious. Christ must be the pivot of her life, and, through Him, the Father and the Holy Spirit must accomplish their work in her. Her concept of Him must be concrete and specific—a woman cannot love in abstraction. Through meditative study of the New Testament and in prayer a sister must come to know the reality of Christ. She cannot love Him until she knows Him. This will mean an intensive and organized study of the New Testament and related readings. Every religious woman should use a good contemporary translation of the New Testament. Its edges should be well-thumbed and its margins filled with personal applications!

Intensive emphasis on knowing Christ personally should be the chief work of the initial formation period in the Postulate, Novitiate, and Juniorate, and should be continued through the daily meditations and spiritual reading of a sister. If a sister has not had the opportunity in her formation to know Christ as a person, she must make up for this lack through her own efforts.

A sister learns to understand Christ's protestations of love for her as a person when He pledges love and security: "Just as the Father loves me, so do I love you. Be sure to hold my love." (John 15:9) She hears His promises of protection and providential concern for her welfare, as well as of rewards and comforts: "As long as you remain with me, and my teaching remains your rule of life, you may ask for anything you wish, and you shall have it." (John 15:7-8) "My own peace is my gift to you." (John 14:27) "Have faith in Me. . . .I want you to be where I shall be." (John 14:1-5)

He also assures her of His personal interest in her and of

His awareness of her needs. "But I have prayed for you personally, that your faith may not fail." (Luke 22:32) After promising a total love, He makes only one demand of her in a plea for reciprocal and complete love: "Love the Lord with your whole heart, mind, soul, and strength; and, besides, love your neighbor as yourself." (Luke 10:27) And in clarifying the practice of this love, He adds, "Whatever love you give to these least brethren of mine, you give to me." (Matthew 25:40) Through experience, a sister comes to know that these are not pious "fervorinos" but influential and meaningful realities in her life. She loves the total Christ —Him and all His people—in the Mystical Body.

The Example of Christ's Love

Christian love takes its impetus from Christ and the manner in which He loved. Christ taught so much about the qualities of love. The religious woman who is in love with Christ must study the principles of His approach in loving others. In general, it is evident from the New Testament that in loving people, Christ was not too concerned about whether they behaved in a way which made them deserving of His love. He loved each one for his individual self. He respected each one's nobility as a human being, so He never "used" anyone to serve His purposes. He bothered only about loving all of them honestly and warmly in human ways which they could understand. He fed them on the mountainside, filled the lake with fish for discouraged fishermen, provided wine for a wedding celebration, embraced babies to the delight of their doting mothers, prepared breakfast on the beach for His close friends, wept at the death of a loved one, publicly accepted the love tokens of a repentant call-girl, breathed life into the dead son of a widowed mother, and forgave the denial of a friend by re-instating him with implicit trust. With great respect for the individual person and with consummate consideration for the feelings of others, Christ accepted them as they were and gently helped them to become what they ought to be. He never forced Himself on anyone or demanded compensation in return, but He tried to make everyone happier and better by loving him. In particular, Christ loved His special friends deeply and intensely—personally and obviously! He was neither ashamed nor afraid to love! In all this He was concerned only about giving—not getting. When others gave love to Him, He warmly accepted it. When His love was appreciated by others, He was gentle and gracious in understanding their compliments. When His love was unnoticed or scorned, He acted as if He wasn't aware of the rejection, even excusing it on grounds of ignorance, and continued to show love to all.

The love of Christ for others is the blueprint for the love a sister gives to people. Christian love, as exemplified by Christ, is expansive and all-inclusive; it is real. Moreover, even though it is all-inclusive, this does not detract, in any way, from the individualized aspect of His love for each person. The love of Christ for others has vision, breadth, depth, and generosity without the hindrances of selfishness and superficiality, which often are evident in human interaction. It is blessed with an honesty and tempered by a tenderness which are concerned only with the good of those loved.

Christian love is concerned about others on a personal basis. Each person is loved for his own sake. Love always concentrates on the good of others. The degree of natural attraction felt towards each person will vary because of personality and temperament differences. Love includes all people, but does not treat them exactly the same, simply because no two persons are exactly alike. Christian love does not require that all people be loved equally or that love be shown to all in the same way.

The element of natural attraction between human beings is good and forms the basis for varying degrees and kinds of love. Christian love requires that all persons be respected for their human dignity and be treated with courteous congeniality. Further, it desires the individual good of each person. There may be people whose actions merit strong disapproval from others because of disagreement of policy, or because those actions are morally wrong. Also, there are those who have undesirable or unattractive personality traits, but one who loves never wishes evil to these people nor condemns them. Rather, one makes efforts to understand and to respect them in a loving way.

Love must be manifested obviously. It cannot be contained. If love exists at all, it will be evident in words and actions. Real love gives a genuineness to people and all they do and say. It is uplifting and tranquil. If love is absent, however, words and actions will be empty of human value even though attempts are made to imitate or to feign real love. Selfish people can be deceptive as they speak the language and simulate the motions of love for their own purposes, but their shallowness makes them vacillating and restive. These people who pretend to love others become increasingly irresponsible and temperamental in their interaction with people. Their inability to withstand the tests of life exposes the dishonesty of their superficiality.

Love must be strong and firm in setting limits, and gentle and persevering in respecting them. Genuine love never hurts the one loved or the one loving; that is, it never damages the integrity or wholeness of a person. Since love cannot really hurt, it may be necessary on occasion to hurt another's feelings by refusing him a request so that he, as a person, may not be injured. It takes a great deal of genuine love to be willing to hurt another's feelings when his good or the common good demands it.

It costs to love others and one must be willing to suffer if he loves. As in all other mature activities in life, one must take risks in loving others. Only a person who is capable of the generosity of complete giving and who is not afraid to be hurt and to make mistakes can really love.

Love usually evokes love in others, and people are always better in some way when they are loving and being loved by others. But it is possible—and often necessary—to love others without receiving love from them in return. Love is patient and understanding in approaching people who do not know how to love because they have never been loved, or who cannot love because they are dominated by fear, guilt, or some other emotional difficulty, or by some false ideology. Because those who love genuinely are primarily concerned only with giving—and not getting—the degree to which they give love is not determined by the amount they get from people in return. It is true, nevertheless, that even mature persons always want a return of the love they give. They too, need to be loved, but they are secure enough to take the risk of being hurt by giving love to others, even when it is not reciprocated by them. The pain of having one's love repeatedly rejected by another, particularly by one to whom love is generously given, should not be underestimated. It is probably the most excruciating of emotional experiences and can be seriously injurious to mental health since it seems to strike at the center of personal security. Such disappointment can be borne realistically and with equanimity only through a genuine faith in God and patient understanding of people.

An emotionally stable sister is fortified in taking these risks by the knowledge that when her love for others is Christ-centered, it is always requited in some way. Christ has promised that He will recognize and reward any love she gives even to the least of His people as if it were given to Him personally. (Matthew 25:40; Mark 9:41) With this assurance of a reciprocity of love from Christ, she can maintain her integrity in bearing the pain when her love for others is unreturned or rejected.

There are two other aspects of the problem of reciprocity in Christian love about which a sister should be concerned. First, a mature sister knows that in loving each person as he is, she also must take love from him in the unique way in which he is able to express it according to his personality. This is part of her acceptance of him as an individual. She allows him to be himself in giving love, ennobling him by her trust and understanding. She gratefully receives his love as he can give it and does not attempt to deprive him of

either his freedom or his integrity by insisting that he sub-
scribe to her demands for particular prescriptions in loving which are contrary to his uniqueness. In the event that
a person needs to learn more mature expressions of love,
she is patient and kind in teaching him.

Secondly, when a sister is offered love by a person to
whom she is not naturally attracted, or by one for whom she
experiences actual repulsion, she may find it very difficult
to be kind. She must make honest efforts to evaluate the
good qualities of these people, so that she can love them for
their own sakes. At the same time, however, she may need
the strength of her faith in Christ's promise and so be able
to show love to these persons sincerely only because she
knows that ultimately she is giving it to Christ and will be
rewarded by Him on that basis.

The Human Need for Affection

Love is mature Christian activity, and only a mature person can really love. Every human being, especially a woman,
needs to show affection. Affection means externally showing
love to another and may be expressed in many ways. Because she understands that love means giving the best in herself, the mature sister knows that she can show her love most
deeply and selflessly by continually giving affection to others
through appreciation, sincerity, loyalty, warm congeniality,
considerateness, understanding, trust, and forgiveness. These
are the substance of love. Habitually to express her genuine
love for others in these ways requires heroic giving of herself, and is the real test of love. Even a selfish sister can

glibly expound to God or to other persons with protestations of superlative love: "willing to give my life for you," "do anything for you." Nevertheless, these are only hollow promises when they are not substantiated by the blessings which characterize mature love. Or, on occasion, an ego-centered sister can boastfully make rash guarantees and striking exhibitions of ardent devotion to "show off" her love for others. A superior may glibly expound the talents of a sister under her direction when she is praised for her accomplishments by the public, and then, on the home front, refuse to give her the loyalty and honesty she deserves as a human being. A sister may promise to initiate great apostolic action for others in a particular assignment and than not be willing to take the consequences of her decisions or to take the risks of being personally hurt. No matter how authentic these spasmodic demonstrations may seem, they are actually ostentatious and cursory expositions founded on the bravado of self-glorification. They are anemic specimens of Christian love and collapse under the inescapable practical pressures of daily living.

According to the laws of love, it is not logical for a sister to pledge the spectacular which is not even remotely probable, when she cannot give the evidence of a love which is immediately possible to her. She must be realistic in her actions of love. Her unaffected honesty in loving others is indelibly Christian to the core. She prepares for the daily offering of gifts of love to God at the altar only after she has purified herself by such acts as: settling arguments with another and apologizing if she has hurt him, considering the feelings of others and attending to their needs, sharing people's joys and encouraging their efforts, and sympathizing with them in their heartaches and overlooking their mistakes. (Matthew 5:29) Such signal love, incorporated meaningfully into daily living, means heroism for a sister apostle. It becomes the purchase price of peace and the absolute authorization of eternal life!

Real kindness, the manifestation of love to another person, is always strong because it takes on the attributes of the sterling love it manifests. It always promotes the good of the one receiving love as well as of the one who gives it. What is actually good for people may not be either what they want or what they think is good for them. It is not always easy to differentiate the one from the other in loving people.

It is possible to use kindness in such a way that it harms others. The person who, in this sense, is too kind is really not honest with himself or others, and therefore often hurts himself and others in some way. Kindness is never weak or catering. It is ever discerning. Love has crystal-clear vision; only selfishness is blind. If a person falsely believes that kindness can never be used to hurt others, he may, on occasion, give things to the person loved which are not good for him, but which only make him "feel good," or which satisfy his emotional demands. Usually there is more human satisfaction in giving kindness than in accepting it. Unless one loves genuinely and selflessly, one may lose focus and be flattered by the generous and grateful responses of those to whom he has been kind, and allow them what they want, rather than what is good for them. Love prudently discriminates between the two courses of action. Pampering a person—that is, giving him what he wants when it is not good for him or when it denies the common good—is not kindness. It may, in fact, be the epitome of unkindness and be detrimental to all people involved. It takes the perceptiveness and strength of genuine love to recognize and to practice the elements of real kindness.

Physical manifestations of affection, such as a kiss or an embrace, can also be signs of love. They never are love itself, however, but when they are given as expressions of a genuine love which really exists, they become meaningful and beautiful symbols of the unselfish love which prompts them. Affectionate acts of any kind are always ennobled or cheapened by the quality of the love which motivates them.

The married woman has a right to physical, as well as psychological, expressions of affection from her husband. In fact, this exchange is necessary to preserve and to develop the love which should exist between a woman and her husband. The married woman satisfies her desires and needs for affection in her love-relationship and companionship with her husband. For her, physical affection is an essential part of the complete self-giving, proper to the sexual act, which should be the sublime expression of real love in marriage. However, her needs for affection, that is, her needs to be shown love, are never exclusively—and not even necessarily—identified with desires for sex.

The religious woman has freely agreed to forego the enjoyment and comfort of legitimate giving and taking of affection proper to marriage. However, she does not thereby relinquish her human right to affection from others nor become exempt from her duty to live Christian love within her religious vocation. Nor does she forfeit any of her capabilities or desires as a woman, so she will not be shocked at herself when she discovers that she, too, sometimes wants others to show affection to her. She will notice, perhaps, that these cravings are more pronounced at certain times, such as during menstruation, or when she experiences illness, fatigue, heartache, or great joy.

These emotional reactions are normal to the periodic physical and psychic changes which take place in her as part of the great plan of God for women. She does not panic when any of these occur, but understands that this is normal because she is a woman. She thanks God for these desires and accepts them according to the prescriptions of her religious vocation by loving others warmly, through congenial companionship in community life, appreciation, considerateness, understanding, and the giving of generous services. Ordinarily, expressions of her love through physical manifestations of affection are not in order, although these may, under certain circumstances, be perfectly proper and necessary. By externalizing herself in these personally rewarding ways, she can keep balance in her life, and become a better apostle of love because she is more of a woman.

In her efforts to love Christ as a person, a sister must beware of the possibility of coming to regard Christ as a man and no more. She may even become preoccupied with the physical aspects of the man. Rather, she must learn to love Christ as a total human person who also is God.

At times, a sister may legalize her desires for physical affection by exchanging it, in imagination, with Christ as a man. In so doing, however, she complicates her life by justifying this transference of affection to Christ. The results can be as disastrous for her emotionally as if she had actualized her imaginings. She may decide that she can afford to be less controlled in this give-and-take of affection with Christ in phantasy because she feels secure on two accounts. First, no one can know what she is imagining, and second, she can readily "supernaturalize" her motives because Christ is a legitimate object of her affection. She can become so involved in phantasy that she experiences all the emotional and physical reactions ordinarily experienced in heterosexual interplay of affection. Since she can construct her phantasies according to her own prescriptions, it will take longer for her to know the natural repugnance normally following illicit indulgence of any kind.

The expressions of love can be intelligently regulated only when a sister really understands love. The desires for affection may be experienced as general needs, or they may be directed to certain persons. Sometimes a sister may interpret the intensity of the desires for physical affection as an indication of the degree of love she has for another person. This may be true, but it is possible, also, that a very intense biological craving for physical affection may not be prompted by love at all, but only by some physiological imbalance or by psychological emptiness resulting from the absence of love.

Sometimes a sister who is not giving of herself in understanding and helping others, but is only getting or withdrawing may substitute the satisfactions of a physical show of affection and feigned psychological closeness for real giving in Christian love. Physical affection, mutually exchanged, can, on occasion, even for a sister be a magnificent expression of real love. To yield to the demands or to forced mani-

festations of affection from another person, however, is a
type of psychological prostitution and a tragic example of
permitting the use of a person for selfish personal advantages. Flippant abuse or calculated use of another's affection
on any level is contemptible dishonesty and constitutes a
base insult to a person's human dignity. Such procedures
contaminate the magnificence of genuine love, and violate
its essential freedom. There is no giving of real love in
counterfeit affection which exists for its own sake, that is,
purely for biological and emotional satisfaction. Under these
circumstances, it can be difficult for a woman to establish a
cut-off between what is only affectional and what is also
sexual. Such expressions of affection often amount to an
intemperance, which if it is not actually lust is closely akin
to it.

With real love for Christ and people as the gauge, the wise
sister develops a sense of Christian prudence and responsibility, rather than a rigid code of minute directives in
selecting her expressions of love to others. Cold formality
kills the warmth of Christian love, and stiff regimentation is
the death blow to its spontaneity. Love is dignified and
ennobled in all its communications through a maturely
regulated and warmly human propriety that is totally Christian.

The Love of Friendship

The fullness of Christian love for a religious woman is
found in friendship. Every mature religious woman needs
to be enriched by the love of genuine and deep human friend-

ship if she is to be a whole person. The magnificence of a well-regulated human friendship is part of her completion as a woman. In fact, it is difficult to visualize total personal development for a sister without it. Genuine friendship is never a detriment to a sister in her love relationship with Christ, but is really an extension and enrichment of it. It is the best human channel through which a sister can come to a more concrete understanding and objective clarification of her true personal relationship with Christ. Furthermore, the love of friendship does not, in any way, exclude a sister's universal love of others. These two aspects of Christian love are simultaneous and supportive. Through real friendship she becomes more humanly fulfilled and is, therefore, more capable of loving Christ as He ought to be loved by her. On the other hand, if she does not also understand and practice universal love for all the people with whom she comes in contact, she can neither maturely accept the responsibilities of a real friendship or consistently maintain balance in appreciating its joys.

Friendship, profound psychological unity of love between two persons, is more intense then the love of good fellowship which exists between persons to whom gratitude is due, or with whom work or recreation is pleasantly accomplished. Each sister, may—in fact, must—cultivate benevolent, amicable relations with many people. In this sense, she should have many friends. It is possible, however, to assume the responsibility for the reciprocal sharing of self with another in the love of a deep friendship—a significant alter-ego relationship—with only a very few persons. The more complete the communication of love in this unique personal involvement, the less frequently is it emotionally possible to repeat.

Friendship is an exchange of love, the complete personal involvement of two people who are so free in their self-possession that they can emote adequately with appropriate adult responses. Only a person who is integrated enough to be comfortable in solitude and to live productively without a friend has the vitality really to love warmly and humanly in friendship. To love another in friendship is to give of oneself, the best one has, in such a way that freedom is not lost nor personal integrity violated. To love and respect a friend means to care so much about him that one could do nothing really to hurt him or oneself.

On occasion, two mature persons who are seeking the good find it in each other and are emotionally attracted by the manner in which this good is expressed through their personalities. They like each other. Each person is loved by the other for what he is. This deep respect, the knowledge and appreciation of individual worth, is the basis of the love of friendship.

For persons who are religious in the Christian sense, and in whom the love of Christ is the great motivating power, any true friendship must, of necessity, be one with this love for Christ. The love of Christ is, as it were, the anchor of a true friendship. It is as if, through the mutual personal attraction, Christ asks two people who personally love Him very much to share their love with each other in and through Him. Thus Christ becomes the focus of this friendship, setting up an affiliation between Himself and the two persons with Christian love as the bond.

Genuine friendship is mutually spontaneous. It is neither

forced nor sudden, but grows gradually and steadily and, perhaps, even imperceptibly, as the innate goodness of each person is discovered and appreciated by the other. This mutual revelation of goodness is an enriched reciprocity because it is stabilized in Christ. Deep friendship cannot be predetermined; laborious efforts to cultivate this depth of love defy its essence and ultimately prevent its development. Real friendship is always a gift freely and mutually given and accepted. Reciprocity of love and esteem of both persons are necessarily involved because love of friendship is much more than hero-worship or one-sided admiration.

People who are real friends preserve their individuality, since the enrichment of friendship emphasizes, rather than discourages, personal identity. There is no need to imitate, to duplicate, or to cultivate identical reactions, even though friends often unconsciously do so. Rather, each person complements the other in a way which increases uniqueness more wonderfully. Friends do not try to change each other. Rather, they share ideas and appreciations in such a way that their personalities are ennobled. Their love makes them better persons. In friendship there must be common experiences and common interests for enrichment. There must be similarity of personal philosophies to facilitate the harmony of relationship, and enough differences to complement and color it.

In the perfect unfolding of self in friendship, a certain compatibility and equality are necessary between friends. (And God is mindful of this in arranging for the bestowal of the gift!) This equality is not so much a sameness, as an ability to develop a oneness—the formation of a new and unique unity—the "us" in friendship. This is a belongingness in which two people learn to live as one in friendship, and wholeheartedly to enjoy the reciprocal give-and-take of their love. The combined strength of the "us" relationship in friendship is stamina for enriched personal living and for more prolific apostolic efforts for a sister. It is a reverent and complete union, and the wonder of it cannot be allowed to wear off, lest it sink to the deadening plateau of taking each other for granted, with all the paralyzing innuendos of self-devotion. This is not the same as selfish possession in which a person attempts to assert proprietorship over another's affections, nor is it immature reliance, in which a person leans on another in emotional helplessness. Further, it is diametrically different from the emotional absorption in which one is shielded from his insecurity while the other is drained of his psychological vigor. There is strength and pro-ductiveness peculiar to the love of friendship which precludes the influence of possessiveness, jealousy, exclusiveness, or temperamentalism so typical of affectional responses based on and sustained by acts of selfishness.

Friends are self-possessed enough consistently to give themselves warmly and freely in desiring their mutual love and in seeking opportunities to manifest it, without the need either to dominate in selfish control or to cling in sentimental dependence. Friends, respectful of each other's personal worth and dignity, arrive at some common understanding in maturely expressing their love.

Love must be told in friendship. The affectionate esteem enjoyed by friends is securely rooted in Christ, and is so profound that it needs more than tangible manifestations. It is expressed best by complete understanding, loyalty, and trust, which actually are more easily felt than verbalized. Love is inventive and creative in revealing itself. Expressions of physical affection between real friends assume the beauty and maturity of the genuine love they express. Close friends maintain orderly perspective in their love relationship, and the delicacy and wonder of the sharing of self with another are preserved because stable emotional reactions, an essential part of deep friendship, are happily accepted and intelligently controlled. Through rational self-government and ordinary common sense, friends keep their love in balance on a warm, but rational Christian level.

Friendship is generous with the extravagance typical of love. It has the courage to take risks in loving, the selflessness to bear its pain, the tenderness to be gentle and kind, and the intensity continually to give and take. Love makes no demands. It never expects more than the one loved is willing to give. Love is free, imposing no binding ties of any kind on the one loved. Friends love each other because they want to, and this freedom is part of the efficacy of the love of friendship. Friends are not afraid to love and to give completely to each other within the limits of Christian friendship. They love warmly and unashamedly because there is security and safety in knowing that each person is giving, not taking. Because of their mutual love, they need each other in a wholesome, real way, and are inclined to use every reasonable opportunity to be together. This concern for preserving and enjoying the love of a friend is not to be confused with the exclusiveness of "ownership" of others. There is stability in genuine love which makes tension, apprehension, or fear negligible. The constant, strong emotional pace of real love in a vital friendship makes for security.

Genuine friendship is eternal. It never dies. In fact, such friendship grows in depth and vision as time goes on. Close friends seek and enjoy many happy and rewarding personal contacts. These contacts should be utilized generously and effectively whenever it is possible; however, they are not essential either to the duration or to the vitality of the friendship. In the event that friends are separated physically, even for long periods of time, their friendship endures. It is, in fact, enriched through their basic affiliation with Christ, and the consequent uninterrupted communication with each other through unfailing loyalty, trust, consideration, and understanding. The affectional bond of friendship can thus be sustained and increased in a very tangible way.

A healthy emotional intimacy exists between friends and makes them sensitive and responsive to each other without an infringement on the privacy of either. Intimacy of spirit—understanding—grows with association and sharing, and gives friends insights into the feelings and reactions of each other. The magnitude of the intimacy of friendship is all encompassing. Nothing is too infinitesimal to be considered or too profound to be penetrated by the understanding of those who love deeply. It cements a love relationship which can make silence comfortable and articulate, words communicative, and companionship happy and rewarding. In such a relationship ostentatious expressions of love are unnecessary, shared confidences respected at all costs, and a sense of redeeming humor an insulation against life's contradictions and sufferings.

Total understanding and unqualified trust are intrinsic to the love of friendship. Loyalty is born of honesty and makes it possible for friends to look to their best personal interests as well as to the common good. The sincerity of friendship prompts friends to help each other with fraternal suggestions, and the shared love offers an indispensable and continuous moral support toward self-improvement. Because of the stability and frankness of its communication, the love of friendship is able to withstand human pressures and misunderstandings without loss.

Genuine friendship is a magnificent blessing of God and can be freely accepted or rejected. But it can never be bartered arbitrarily across the counters of self-interest and utility.

This special kind of dialogue between two emotionally balanced people is, in many ways, a mystery, overwhelming and awesome at times, an experience that eludes description. It gives continual joy because it is one of the greatest human blessings, and produces peace because it is free and unselfish. It is personally fulfilling because it is the most genuinely refined human act.

Friendship, thus understood, is the culmination of love on the human level. It has its prototype in the love of Christ for His friends, and its measure in the unbounded expanse of that love. There is, therefore, no limit to giving in real love of friendship. This deep love of friendship has its source in a mutual love-relationship with Christ and a common commitment to His cause.

Obstacles to the
Practice of Christian Love

The Influence of False Theories

If a sister has not had satisfactory developmental experiences in her early life or for some other reason has not progressed emotionally beyond the level of childhood or adolescence, she will have difficulty loving in religious life. It may also happen that a sister who has learned to love before she came to the convent suffers psychological damage from the false ideologies presented to her in the initial preparation for religious life.

The Jansenistic approach to living the religious life, with its severe condemnations of human nature and its rigid overemphasis on a false morality, which has only too frequently colored the traditional formation of sisters in the past, may be partially responsible for this. The overtones and influences of such a philosophy are not easily or quickly eradicated from conventual living.

Much of traditional religious life has been heavy with negative explanations, interpretations, and recommendations. Often, it was considered virtuous for sisters to "crush their humanness" and to cultivate a cold indifference in "living for God alone," without any practical understanding of the fact that a Christian's love for God is, by Divine prescription, measured by his love for people. Love was confused with sensuality, chastity was identified with abstention from affection, and conventual virtue was described as passivity. Sisters were directed to silent endurance in uninterrupted suffering as the application of "take up your cross and follow Me", and physical isolation from the "evil world" was regarded as holy indifference.

If sisters should attempt to live the counsels in religious life according to these directions they must denounce and condemn their humanness, leave their talents undeveloped, become as uninterested in people as possible, and reduce themselves to a state of psychological inertia. The less human they could become, the holier they were adjudged.

Woman cannot live in an emotional vacuum. A sister merely exists, and eventually becomes less-than-human, when she attempts to create a psychological void for herself by insisting that she needs no one or in cultivating a cold disinterestedness in people. These refusals to love may be partially protective for her, but she can never successfully rationalize them with pious "fervorinos" or an erroneous philosophy of life.

If a sister is to become a saint as she is supposed to be, she must become more wonderfully human as she grows older. But, if she has been formed by a false philosophy in her youth, it is difficult for her to revamp her life, even when she is convinced of the need for change. At best, human attitudes and convictions change slowly and only with consistent effort. If a sister has been formed in a moralistic cult of legalism with all its implications of guilt and self-penalization, it is difficult for her to feel free in living as a human being.

The Power of Unhealthy Fears

It may be well to look at some of the problems involved

here for sisters. The sister, who, for some reason, is not an adult psychologically will be insecure and diffident. Fear will be the most devastating factor in deterring her from the practice of Christian love. She is threatened and so she will have many fears of varying kinds and degrees. There is no end to the list of fears which can plague a religious woman. Since the immature sister is unable correctly to evaluate herself, she does not know who she is, and her greatest fear is that she will not be loved and accepted for herself. Since she cannot accept herself, she has little, if any, self-confidence. Unreasonable fear makes her extremely self-centered and self-conscious. It dominates her life, so that self and all its concerns—not Christ and His people—are the center of her attention. Fear makes her tense and inflexible and kills all possibility of loving, since unreasonable fear and love cannot coexist. Sometimes a sister—even a mature sister—is afraid to give and to take love even when it is what she needs and desires more than anything else.

A sister who is habitually fearful is afraid of making mistakes, of what others will think and say of her, of being rejected, of suffering ridicule, of committing sin, and of being a bad Religious. She is afraid to get old, to form an opinion—much less to express it—to use her talents, and to love others. She is afraid of herself and of everyone else. Sometimes she is afraid of fear, of being unsuccessful, of illness, of being unloved, of dying—and mostly of living. Often she is just afraid. Frequently, she feels lonely and empty. She is frustrated and restless, suspicious and uncooperative, and unfriendly and anxious. She attempts to make substitutions for loving and looks to various avenues of distractions for consolation in her empty life. She may indulge in sensuous pleasures of eating intemperately, or of wasting time in inconsequential pursuits, or in the feverish flurry of activism, attempting to fill her emptiness with excessive work, reading, hobbies, or in tending to the affairs of others—anything to keep busy physically. She may also develop competence in adhering to the letter of conventual routine and rule to compensate for the lack of imagination and spirit in her life. It is possible that she will look for "safety" from herself and others by withdrawing from people and living in a world of her own. She may attempt to achieve status with others by boasting of her real or imaginary accomplishments, or by playing the role of the reformer.

The Escape Into Phantasy

Powers of imagination are a gift of God to human beings. Great apostolic action and creativity are generated in imagination by a mature sister. Like all human powers, however, it serves best when wisely regulated. The sister who is not loving usually has an undisciplined imagination. It is one of the most lively and fertile compensations she has, because there she can have life as she wants it, when she can no longer endure it as it is, or face it responsibly as she ought. The area of phantasy is probably the most popular—and depersonalizing—escapism used by sisters.

When a sister does not face reality in living, she actually functions as if she were living in a make-believe world, returning psychologically to certain aspects of her childhood when she could suddenly turn reality off and on with only a twist of the imagination. It is possible for her to construct a well-organized system of false gods according to whose direction and in whose honor she motivates her life. Primarily, she loves herself rather than God and people. She worships the gods of human respect, popularity, comfort and convenience, and takes flight, in imagination, from the actual facts of life and retreats to a realm of pretension which can adequately be symbolized by a birdhouse. The metaphoric comparison seems apt in the sense that the confusion resulting from living habitually in imagination, psychologically cripples a human being in much the same way that the restriction of living in a real birdhouse would physically incapacitate him. The space there is grossly curtailed, and vision from the dwarfed opening is reduced to pinpoint proportions, so emotional discomfort prevails and true facts are obscured, misconstrued, or completely absent.

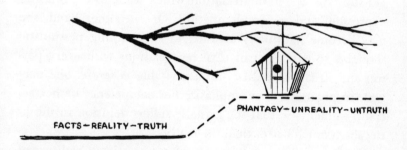

PHANTASY–UNREALITY–UNTRUTH

FACTS–REALITY–TRUTH

There are many ways in which a sister can make unrealistic approaches to life's conflicts and problems after she has escaped from reality and sought refuge in her phantasy birdhouse. Usually the self-centered person finds ego comfort temporarily while she is in the birdhouse. Nevertheless, this is a real danger for a sister because she can indulge in this selfish thinking undetected. If a bell would tinkle in community living every time a sister left reality, it can safely be predicted that life in some convents would be a fairly musical affair! A further complication of unrealistic living lies in the fact that the daydream atmosphere may become so comfortable for a sister, that she finds it difficult to withstand the blast of reality and so, in self-defense, is compelled to retreat to phantasy rather permanently.

In the domain of phantasy, it is possible for a sister to concentrate on herself in such a way that she magnifies all that happens to her, coloring it to her advantage, or to imagine things which have never really happened at all. If she chooses, she can be the suffering heroine in any imaginary drama, and, as a consequence, she feels sorry for herself and condemns others. It is likely, too, that she may engage in a sadistic type of self-depreciation which leads to debilitating depression and self-condemnation. On the other hand, she may become habitually attuned to entertaining pessimistic thoughts so that she can turn her relations with every person and situation in life into a veritable *miserere*. She may also, in phantasy, over-emphasize her competence or her accomplishments so that she actually suffers delusion in thinking she is much better than she really is.

To show how the dynamics of phantastic unreality can enter into daily living, consider the example of a sister who has very successfully taught sixth grade in a small town school for five years. She has been a cooperative and congenial community member, and now receives an Obedience from her Mother Superior to teach fourth grade in a large suburban school. These are the facts, and they prompt the sister to accept the new appointment with resignation and challenge her to do the same good work in the new setting.

Sister, however, has not habituated herself to realistic living. In fact, she is quite unaware that she has established an influential system of false gods in her life. Instead of seeing and accepting the facts as they are, therefore, she takes off to the phantasy birdhouse, and begins to think: "Why did I have to be transferred? . . . I wonder if they got me out of that other school? . . . I remember that sometimes Sister X seemed cold to me . . . I'll bet she did it! . . . They must be punishing me for something, otherwise I wouldn't have been assigned to a lower grade . . . They are jealous of me. . . . I was having too much success (and you really can't be successful in the convent!) . . . They just want me to fail!" And *ad infinitum*—the unrealistic, untrue thoughts tumble one after the other through the sister's mind, making her most uncomfortable and unhappy because now she has convinced herself that this is the actual situation.

Where is the opportunity for apostolic love to glow when her spirits are withered by self-pity? It never occurs to her that if the Superior took time to tell her the reason, it would simply be because she wanted sister to be within a ten-minute ride of St. Ethelreda College, so she could attend Saturday classes and complete her work for a degree this coming semester. How balancing the truth could be if only sister were able to see it!

Another pertinent example is Sister A who enthusiastically, and even a bit dogmatically, suggests at the community recreation, when the sisters are discussing the site of the next community picnic, that they go to St. Rufina's shrine about 200 miles away. Her further recommendations roll in this order: they could charter a bus . . . leave the convent about 6:30 a.m. after a 5 a.m. Mass and a hurried breakfast . . . make the 4½ hour trip . . . have lunch on the lawn . . . pay due respect to good St. Rufina by chanting the office (well! at least part of it!) in front of the statue . . . and begin the trip home again. Understandably, the community doesn't share her enthusiasm for a "day of relaxation away from home," and they are frank and unanimous in telling her so as they enumerate their objections. Majority opinion rules (as it should in such cases) and the community—all but Sister A—goes to Flannigan's cottage on Lake Savannah twenty miles away to enjoy a day of fishing, wading, swimming, softball, bridge, and a typical picnic lunch. These are the facts. And, after all, opinions and tastes do vary!

Things could have been amicably settled even for Sister A had she realistically evaluated the situation. Instead, she takes off to her phantasy birdhouse where things, unhappily for her, are the way she makes them. Now the vision she sees through the restricted birdhouse opening is this: "I've been working for God and this Community for 35 years . . . and I am not accepted in spite of all I've done . . . all I have to do is to make a suggestion and it is coldly rejected . . . and they don't want me because they don't want my ideas . . . they would give up a holy pilgrimage to a shrine of note for the worldliness of a lake picnic (she forgot that God made the lake and the fishes, and man the shrine!) . . . I'm so crushed by this . . . I'll stay out of their way as long as they don't want me . . . I won't go to the picnic. . . ."

With this backdrop, Sister A is sullenly silent, stays home from the picnic, and mopes in her room (or possibly even makes a holy hour in the chapel!). Simultaneously, she is totally miserable and even dislikes herself for her conduct, but can't bring herself to do anything about it. And so, in her phantasy, Sister A remains a foreigner to Christian love.

Frequent indulgence in this type of phantastic day-dreaming can dull a sister's objectivity so that she becomes unable to distinguish between what is real and what is only imagined. Phantasy living of some kind is the foundation for all forms of worldliness: untruthfulness, rationalization, uncharitableness of all kinds. A sister's general well-being, as well as the cause of charity, are jeopardized when she allows these sentiments to dominate her personal life and her interaction with people. Such self-centered existence is not normal. It is a psychological anemia which drains her strength as a Christian woman, destroys her mental health, and prevents her from coping with life intelligently. When she does not see herself in true perspective, she becomes either arrogant and unappreciative of the accomplishments of others, or unhappy and unproductive in her efforts to love others. All of these reduce her potential as a sister apostle. Usually, a system of false references is established by a sister unwittingly, and surely without malice or forethought. Precisely because it is so subtle, it often goes unperceived by a sister until a habit has been formed and her life is significantly influenced by it.

In life there are many obstacles to the goals which a sister seeks. It rains when she has planned a picnic; she has a splitting headache the day she must take a semester examination in a graduate course; she has a class which is not readily motivated to learn; she is appointed to live with a sister for whom she has a pronounced aversion; or her heart is numb in sharing the terminal illness of a friend. Usually a sister experiences some feeling of dissatisfaction, disappointment, annoyance, or futility when the attainment of a desired goal is obstructed by an obstacle. The sister who is an adult Christian finds God in these necessary purifying experiences and capitalizes on them as invaluable learning opportunities. When she learns to handle these situations by facing reality maturely, she will be able to accept these frustrations with balance, but not without pain. She will, however, reduce or eliminate the human tensions which otherwise arise from these experiences.

Thought control is extremely important in regulating phantasy life. When a sister resorts to unreal or immature actions because of worshipping false gods in phantasy, she is always motivated in some way—to win affection, to get recognition, to avoid embarrassment, to lessen the pain of emptiness, or to obtain a similar end. There is always a reason why she acts as she does. Because she perceives and appraises her situation in an unreal way, she is moved to use unrealistic means to solve her problems. This only produces more conflict in her life, and she again resorts to these totally inadequate means of solving them. Thus the cycle is repeated until, unfortunately, it becomes a habitual pattern of living.

Often a sister is unaware of these dynamics in the sense that she does not see any connection between her conflicts and the method she chooses to settle them. For instance, a sister knows that frequently she talks piously about the merits of religious life. However, she does not see that it is to cover up the guilt she feels because she is not saying prescribed prayers regularly or attentively.

On the other hand, another sister may adhere to conventual formalities with unfailing zeal, merely to compensate for the fact that she is consistently critical in her interactions with others. Yet another sister may know that she is unfair in habitually judging a person rashly and harshly, but may not realize that these judgments really are projected evaluations of herself, and are prompted by the self-condemnation which results from her deliberate indulgence of jealousy.

Usually when a sister does not accept reality as it exists in herself and in her environment, she develops inferiority feelings and feelings of inadequacy, if she does not already have them. These feelings come from real or imagined personal deficiencies or inadequacies. This sister does not have a good self-concept—she does not know who she is. She tends to form her opinion of herself by what she feels others think of her rather than by what she really is. Sometimes a sister cultivates these feelings and thoughts of inadequacy— thinking, erroneously, of course, that it is humility.

A sister who suffers from feelings of inferiority is plagued by the consequences thereof: over-sensitivity to criticism which makes her also over-responsive to flattery; hypercritical attitude by which she tends always to blame others; feelings of guilt, uselessness, and insecurity which make her react hesitantly—and perhaps, even cowardly—to competition; general tendency to seclusiveness, shyness, or timidity which make her build a psychological wall around herself for protection; and boastfulness about the things she can do in an effort to acquire some semblance of self-esteem.

When a sister refuses to be a real person, she can squander much valuable time in living the love of her commitment. She can procrastinate, letting things go so she doesn't have to take action. She may be so afraid of what others will say of her that she cannot assume either the initiative to make decisions or the responsibility for their consequences. She can get so engrossed in work by taking on more jobs than is reasonable that she doesn't have time to face problems realistically or to enjoy life humanly. For her, happiness is a frivolity to be avoided! She becomes a slave to work, estimating her love of God by time-clocks of activity, rather than by an eye-level contact with the people He loves. Also, she may forget that every generation has its "fling," and that constant reference to the "good old days" may be just an excuse for refusal to face the facts of today's jet age! Likewise, she may find herself consistently justifying her conduct by giving her own reasons, rather than the right ones. She may complacently drown her inadequacies in the group, living on the reputation of the Community, rather than making serious efforts to become a saint of love in her own right!

The Desperation of Jealous Love

The fearful sister does not know how to love and is suffocating in her emotional emptiness, so she "clings" to someone or something for security. When she becomes possessive, she is necessarily jealous. Jealousy stems from a peculiar combination of self-centeredness and insecurity. Because she is desperate for love the jealous sister sees herself in the hub of things, and it usually never occurs to her that this might not be the proper perspective. She sees life as an overwhelming threat. If her supremacy in the affection of another is challenged, or her security in her job, or the recognition of her talents, she will become angry and mistrustful because she is afraid. In other words, a jealous person sees love as a competition, and if she cannot hold the supreme affectional position—the "exclusively yours" status—in the life of another to whom she is attracted, she becomes frightened. She is so threatened that she may not even bother to discover whether the feeling is mutual or take time to evaluate the love that is being shown to her, but resorts to typically adolescent reactions of excessive tears, cynicism, coldness, or some other form of hypersensitiveness.

A jealous sister may pout and sulk and expect her victim to seek her out to discover what is the matter. The jealous person seems to find some particular emotional gratification in the fact that the other person "loves me enough to come after me." For the jealous person, there seems to be some magic alleviation for emotional emptiness in the dynamics of the "quarrel-and-make-up" process. The delusion of jealousy directs her to say "If I didn't really love you, I wouldn't be jealous." But the truth is, "If I really loved you, I couldn't be jealous," because jealousy is a result of selfish possession, and genuine love never binds. It is free. There are no restrictive ties of any kind in genuine love.

Jealousy is ruthless and is deterred by nothing in its efforts to gain satisfaction. When others are complimented,

for instance, a jealous sister may consider herself slighted
and unloved and become moody and self-pitying. Also,
when she knows that someone to whom she is attracted has
other friends, she may feel cheated of what she considers her
affectional rights. She seriously lacks the faith in herself
which would make her confident in loving, so even repeated
assurances that she is loved are not permanently comforting
or satisfying to her. On occasion, she may resort to almost
cruelly unreasonable attacks on the person loved. It is possible that sometimes the best motives can be warped by
incredible misinterpretations; the most noble actions can be
stripped of their value by suspicious judgments; the warmth
of friendship can be frozen by cynical coldness; the spontaneity of real love can be withered by hurting personal denunciations; and, eventually, the vitality of love can be substantially damaged by continual onslaughts of jealousy.

Likewise, this sister may direct her efforts to a peculiar
brand of revenge, typical of real jealousy, through open or
disguised attempts to destroy the reputation of the person
she sees as a rival. Even though these reactions may appear
as meanness, they usually are not. They may be prompted
by a state of near panic resulting from almost overpower-
ing desires for certainty that she is loved for herself. Much
pain comes to a jealous sister who, even against her better
judgment and sincere wishes, is driven to these apparently
contradictory actions. She needs understanding help in building the essential trust necessary to love and to accept the love
of another person.

It is psychologically interesting that often jealousy indulges
in a great game of pretend. It may wear masks of magna-

nimity and generosity as it parades as love. It can even be the motivation for intrinsically good actions. A sister may rationalize her jealousy by speaking freely, and convincingly, about the exact opposite of what she is and feels. For example, a sister who is jealously possessive of another person, may speak about her great feelings of friendship and her willingness to "share" that person with others, or she may give homilies on her emotional independence in "not needing anyone." Incidentally, the sister who boasts "I don't need anyone's love—I can live for God alone" is "whistling in the dark" because she is starving from emotional malnutrition. She forgets that God chooses to identify Himself so closely with people that love for Him can be shown by loving them. In this sense, not even God can stand the attempted isolation of an "only God and me" relationship and the sister finds herself pathetically alone. If she is really to accept God at all, she must also accept all people whom He loves. It is likely that when someone asks a jealous sister to share a confidence or to participate in a task, she must publicize the fact. Then others will know that she has established a "close" bond with someone and that is a boost to her *ego* Or a sister can be very generous to others, as a superior is in giving things to the sisters under her direction; or as a sister teacher is in being particularly congenial to certain students; or as a sister nurse is untiringly devoted to a particular patient—all for selfish reasons. It is possible that such actions are really an effort to "buy" the affection of other people. The jealous sister thus obligates people to gratitude in return for the favors she does for them. Only genuine love can perforate sham like this!

The jealous sister is uncomfortably self-conscious and when someone gives attention to her, this gnawing self-awareness is alleviated and she feels better. She suffers the same desperation as a drowning person who grasps at anything for preservation. This is the reason she "clings" so tenaciously and unreasonably to people or to jobs as her source of security.

Other sisters may dominate things rather than people. For instance, the sister cook who would not think of interacting warmly with other persons, puts a psychological fence around the convent kitchen, and figuratively labels it "mine," so the other sisters cannot safely and freely enter. She possesses the place of her work. The sister teacher may "own" certain equipment or books that no one else may touch because these symbolize a power that she must jealously guard. A sister may jealously refuse to relinquish a position or an office when requested to do so by a superior, or when she can no longer competently function in that capacity.

The sister who finds it necessary regularly to retire very late, or to absent herself from the community recreation, or to skip the noon lunch because she refuses assistance with her job, stubbornly insisting on "doing her own work," may be jealously clinging to this work as a source of personal security or satisfaction. Or the sister who guards her cleaning charge in the convent reception rooms as if it were a rare museum piece, may be jealous of her proprietorship of this assignment. The total domination of a situation seems to anesthetize the misery of insecurity for such Religious.

Jealousy, in any form, can prompt actions that seem so small, so ignoble, that those who allow it to empower them feel particularly embarrassed and guilty, and seldom are willing to admit it even to themselves. This is the reason why jealous people are often the most deluded about their condition.

Fear and phantasy do not carry the same social stigma for a sister as jealousy, but they are equally destructive of her personal balance and her apostleship. In fact, they can be more treacherous, precisely because they are not so obviously baffling and repulsive to her. She may not realize that continued indulgence in fear or phantasy can be dangerous obstacles to Christian love. Therefore, while a sister may be willing to acknowledge the influence of fear or phantasy on her actions, she tends to rationalize them easily, to disregard them as of little consequence without making serious efforts to combat them. In other words, it is easier to "get by" with fear and phantasy than with jealousy, but, in the end, the damage to personal integrity may be greater.

Once a sister realizes the effects of jealousy, fear, or phantasy she usually has feelings of futile helplessness and disturbing restlessness. She knows no peace. She experiences gnawing regret because of her mistakes, and may desire to be relieved of these anxieties. Generally, however, she is unable to face the facts frankly. Therefore, while she makes resolutions to reform, she does not follow them through effectively until she is miserable enough to seek help.

Such a sister needs the help of an understanding, competent person who can help her to view life more rationally. She must resolutely begin a program of rehabilitation by a staunch willingness to face her problems honestly and to develop tenacity of purpose in confronting them. Unqualified admission of these deviations and earnest determination to do something about them are the prerequisites for action. A sister will gradually see that jealousy, fear, and phantasy are her reactions when she deliberately or inadvertently imagines situations in which she is seeking her own good rather than that of others. Furthermore, she will recognize that she often quite deliberately harbors these phantasies and feelings and permits them to regulate her actions.

With assistance, she can develop healthy self-acceptance and learn to be patient and honest with herself so she can live comfortably with reality. In establishing this realistic perspective, she will be firm and consistent in controlling her thoughts. She must also be alert and discerning in differentiating between what she only feels and thinks and what she really knows to be objectively true. She will find it imperative to direct her actions adamantly by rational conclusions even when her emotional reactions are not in harmony with them. She cannot accomplish this unless she is sincere in asking for and using God's help. She must be willing to take the risk of making mistakes as she learns a new approach to life. Further, she will make herself responsible for a true apostolic dedication in which she can expend her energies and interests productively and selflessly. Thus, she will be too busy with the cardinal concerns of life to squander time unrealistically. She will become free in dealing with the genuine in life, and will come to know wholesome Christian security.

The battle to overcome jealousy, fear, or phantasy is long and difficult. Persistent efforts to regulate their influence demand hard work and are not always comfortable. Eventually, however, they provide liberating release from the tyranny of emotional living, and the resulting rewards of peace and wholeness are highly satisfying.

The Confusion Surrounding Unordered Attachments

The sister who is not loving and being loved adequately may find that the fundamental need to be loved by others and to be "special" to somebody, just because she is herself, is intensified. For some reason—the inability to love effectively as an adult, denial of opportunity to love in community life, or the effects of fear and rejection—this sister will be literally starved for love.

She is psychologically desperate in the hurt of this emotional destitution, and in her attempts to survive this painful experience, she may become involved in a relationship which is commonly known in conventual circles as a "particular friendship." "Particular friendship" is one of the most feared and misunderstood bogies of religious life for women. Sisters, in general, are afraid of this term because they don't know exactly what it is. They are not sufficiently informed either about its meaning or its implication. Therefore, since they do not know either how to recognize or how to avoid these unordered attachments, they tend to be wary of all friendly relationships with people, including genuine friendships.

The term "particular friendship" is not only misleading, but totally incorrect. It is a gross misnomer for two reasons: first, the condition it designates is not comparable to real friendship in any way; second, essentially, every genuine friendship must be particular, so it is unnecessary to specify this quality in speaking of friendship. It is particularly important for sisters to understand this, especially those who look askance at friendships as if they were a creation of the devil instead of a blessing of God, or who insist on defining "universal love" in terms of treating everyone alike, or of loving all people to the same degree. These sisters justify their point of view by pointing out that since all friendship is particular, it must also be exclusive, and therefore anathema in religious life. This is a classic conventual heresy which generates suspicion and uncharitableness and works immeasurable havoc in community living.

In "particular friendship" the bond of interpersonal cohesion between two or more people is centered in some form of selfishness rather than in the love of Christ and the mutual love of the persons concerned as is true in genuine friendship. In fact, people do not need to know each other really in this type of relationship, hence time and real self-sharing are not important elements.

Traditionally, "particular friendship" has been regarded only as a relationship between two people which violates chastity. Actually, however, while violations of chastity may be part of a "particular friendship," they need not be. Such relationships may also be based on infractions of charity, which are not only regrettably unchristian, but destructive to personal happiness and to community and apostolic life for sisters. Contrary to popular conventual opinion, "particular friendship" is essentially a violation of Christian charity in which the parties involved mutually restrict their attention and interest to their selfish satisfactions, and thus deny themselves the freedom and the time to love all people generously. During this time, Christ is not the focus of a sister's life.

"Particular friendship" is an unordered attachment which may assume several forms, such as a sensual infatuation, a sexual affiliation, a cult of criticism, or a combination of all these states. Community life and the spirit of religious living are not only damaged but may be completely destroyed by this type of exclusive and possessive interpersonal communication. Apostolic enthusiasm cools and professional proficiency deteriorates. Consideration for the common good vanishes and the cause of Christ is impeded.

The sister who does not love tends to respond demonstratively and superlatively when anyone shows her any preference. She does not have the ability critically to appraise the responses of others to her, so she may be so overcome by emotional adulation of the "good-feeling-around-the-heart" variety, when someone notices her, that she topples psychologically. Since she is unable to make an honest evaluation of these attentions, especially if they are from someone to whom she is strongly attracted naturally, her spurts of emotional reactions towards these people are superficial.

She is inclined to become infatuated and to get "crushes" on people easily. Since she is still an adolescent psychologically, her emotions soar high at the slightest provocation and drop as rapidly and easily. She is especially responsive to flattery. These surface reactions need not be based on truth to be satisfying to her. She can take a grain of truth and magnify it in phantasy to represent the proportion of emotional depth she wants, and often she cannot distinguish between reality and phantasy.

This sister is hungry for affection, and in the desperation of her emotional deprivation, she may set up an exclusive relationship with another person—a sister or a lay person—which is both time consuming and thought absorbing. Physical presence, the only thread of assurance in this type of relationship, is absolutely necessary to maintain this association, so the victims seek many opportunities to meet privately and secretly.

The sister who is immature usually is fickle in loving. She can concentrate only on the tangible satisfactions of the affection she gets, probably because her need of it is so great. Since she is emotionally shallow, she easily becomes fascinated by the affective responses of another to her. Her approach to love can be deceptive since it may have a certain breadth and intensity, but very little depth and sincerity. Her demonstrations of love are empty and sentimental, but may be camouflaged well as real love. They are, however, neither really true nor lasting. Her sentiments vacillate arbitrarily, so she can quite easily terminate her affection for one person and, without significant regret, transfer it to another with equal fervor. Her need for affection is the directive for all of her love relationships.

"Thinking-of-you-all-the-time", domination of the time of a person, demands for complete and exclusive claim to affection, constant checking on actions, forced invasion of personal privacy are part of the excesses involved in the attempt to possess another. Neglecting duty, excluding others from charity, avoiding family and friends, and using prayer time to indulge phantastic day dreams of the loved one can be other effects of these immature emotional involvements.

In spite of ardent promises of fidelity and profuse imitations of love, affectional relations based on selfishness of any kind really will not stand the test of physical separation. The gnawing restlessness for physical possession of a person and the haunting thought absorption kills a sister's peace of mind and drains her strength as an apostle. Another consequence of these infatuations is the proprietorship one person exerts over the other. Such "use" continues as long as it is profitable to them—as long as they get the satisfaction they want. Their chief attraction is what they get, not what they give. And the personal worth of the individuals involved is not their prime concern even if they make themselves think it is. This is an ideal setting for jealousy and all its ramifications.

The substantial comforts of understanding, patience, forgiveness, loyalty, and constancy, the affectionate signs of real love, are unknown qualities in these superficial affiliations. It must be noted, too, that in an unordered relationship the needs for physical contact, mental absorption, and personal possession result from surface emotional elation and insecurity, and deplete the psychological vigor of those involved. This is different from a real friendship where the prevailing consciousness of a friend and the valid need for frequent personal contact, prompted by genuine and deep love, are charged with the potency of peace and joy. Unlike the counterfeit friendship, real friendship makes a sister strong and more capable of a whole apostolic service. It can not only survive physical separation, and the inevitable difficulties of human interaction, but can become intensified and deepened because of it. In genuine friendship, the total mutual giving is always free. Selfish expedience and personal convenience have no part in the love of real friends. Their mutual love is all giving.

Since there is no solid bond of love in their relationship, people who are infatuated flatter each other and create emotional elation for themselves by mimicing the words and actions of genuine love without ever giving the real in themselves. It is possible that people involved in such a relationship never really reveal themselves to each other. They may even make specific efforts to avoid this self-exposition. Surface contacts are safe since they involve no risks or inconveniences. Eventually these people may follow natural inclinations blindly and selfishly demand physical expressions of affection, not as signs of love, but as balm for insecurity and food for emotional satisfaction. They see these expressions as a clinching bond of affiliation—possibly the only one they can understand or are interested in establishing at the time. On the contrary, particularly when sisters are concerned, they may discreetly and conscientiously avoid any display of physical affection, vainly making this the grounds of justification for their immature and surface attempts to love. Efforts may also be made to imitate real closeness through a superficial sharing of confidences and interests. This becomes the externalization of their sentiments to one another. They may confide personal matters to each other, but actually they never are capable of sharing themselves in a real way.

When these surface overtures peculiar to infatuations are attended by references to God, people who are superficially enamored of each other feel they have developed a "spiritual friendship." This is seen by them as a safety zone. It can, however, be a subtle and deceptive psychological trap for unsuspecting victims, especially if they are religious women. By capitalizing on the "supernatural" aspect of their relationship, they may successfully justify it to themselves and carry on the delusion for a long time. The affection exchanged may simulate ardor and sincerity, but basically it exists for its own comfort and satisfaction and lacks the strength and beauty of genuine love. The emotional emptiness is relieved, at least for the time being. The affection is rationalized as mutual love, which, in phantasy, one or both persons have convinced themselves exists. This is particularly true if there is no need for intimate and continual contact in which there is danger of having to expose themselves to each other. Pseudo-love thrives on emotionally toned reassurances of any kind, but usually collapses completely in the face of life's genuine tests.

The artificiality of this situation gradually produces unrest and disillusionment. As is the case in every unreasonable or abusive use of God's gifts, there is no limit to the problems which can originate in a fertile imagination which is set off adequately by excessive and unreal affection. It is like pouring gasoline on a fire. The margin between a sensual infatuation, particularly one of any duration, and a sexual affiliation is negligible, and the fawning mutual interchange of admiration of the hero-worship variety is the first step to an unsatisfying brand of insincerity.

Excessive and illicit indulgence in physical demonstrations of affection, or duplicity in protesting love only to make others "feel good" and to elicit their insincere praise in return, like intemperance of any kind, readily lead to some degree of self-disgust and perhaps even to some aversion also for the other person. So these relationships, at best, are temporary and frustrating to those who engage in them. Fundamentally, they are temperamental and unenduring. They are not free, but slavishly demanding, so they do not bring real peace.

Even as they indulge in these deviations, sisters who are plagued by fear and cannot love, who seek affection as compensation for loneliness, or who are incapable of loving maturely, sincerely wish to be freed from them. They do not want to live this way. Often they may not see the connection between their actions and their inability to love. Such sisters really want to love and to be loved properly and they must be given credit for their good intentions and their willingness to rectify their mistakes. If necessary, they must be taught how to love, or be permitted to love in normal, human living in community and apostolic life. Sisters who really know how to love do not trade the real happiness of genuine love for the insipid and unsatisfying pleasures of emotional excesses.

A sister who becomes involved in an unordered attachment may actually be only desiring and seeking real affection, and not sexual or sensual pleasure at all. She may be most sincere in thinking she is really loving. If a sister finds herself involved in this type of superficiality, she will, undoubtedly, be confused and distressed, and possibly experience some guilt and/or self-aversion. She may look for some means of escape.

A sister who finds herself confronted with this problem

may feel she needs help in balancing her emotional life or in learning how to love maturely. She should not be shocked at herself, or engage in self-condemnation. This has occurred because she is a human woman, so she should face the facts quietly and with understanding, and make concentrated efforts to regulate her affectional responses.

A good confessor, who not only sees moral implications, but also understands the psychological dimensions of this situation for the sister as a woman, can be of great assistance to her. A sister may, however, need additional assistance. Ideally, professional help should be available to her if she needs it. If it is not, however, a sister must be most careful and prudent in discussing her problem with another person. This is a situation not ordinarily understood by most sisters, and to discuss it with someone who will not understand or who is scandalized by it will only aggravate the problem for her. Besides, a sister has a right to preserve her good name, and also the obligation to protect that of other persons involved.

It may be that a sister feels there is no one whom she can trust enough to speak freely about this matter. If so, it is usually better for her to do the best she can to resolve the problem with only the help of her confessor, rather than to risk a damaging violation of confidence or a harmful lack of understanding on the part of the confidant.

Warmth in human interaction is never "particular friendship," but those sisters who have set out on a path of determined aloofness may be inclined to brand it so. Sisters may never judge others in these matters. The possibility of excess in the feeling aspects of love is no excuse for refusing to love. Sisters usually do not refuse to eat at least three or four times a day, even though by doing so, they expose themselves to the danger of over-indulgence. They know how to exert intelligent control. It is better, by far, to make mistakes and, in the process, learn really to love, than to remain inhumanly cold out of fear of taking the risks involved. Two sisters should not be made to feel guilty when they enjoy each other's company in community life. Sisters should enjoy being together, whether in work or in recreation, and *laudates* of thanksgiving should be chanted when congenial relations do exist among sisters.

Ordinarily, sisters think only of the sensual and sexual relationship as a "particular friendship". But it is possible that an unordered attachment is established when a cult of uncharitableness develops as the bond of communication between two or more sisters or between a sister and a lay person. Some form of perpetual criticism, habitual complaining or grumbling may form the basis for the affiliation. Everyone who does not agree with them falls beneath their lashes of criticism. No one is safe with them. Reputations are destroyed or damaged with abandon. Situations are exaggerated or misrepresented. Uncharitableness of some form is the favorite pastime of such cliques, and the members can become so habituated to it that they do it quite spontaneously. When there are no problems, they concoct them, and phantasy takes care of the rest. Truth is sacrificed to their purposes. Often, they scrupulously avoid ever touching each other physically, for fear of having a "particular friendship."

Usually these sisters are the "hard" individuals who "don't need anyone," but who sit in righteous condemnation and judgment over all who love genuinely. To establish love as a crime is their conventual paradox. Their distorted understanding of the meaning of Christian love prompts them to impute questionable motives to the actions of sisters who love. Little do they realize that sins against charity often are more devastating than sins against chastity, both to those who are guilty of them and to those whom they victimize. While they can never be approved, it must be understood that initial failures of impurity as implied in the traditional concept of particular friendship do stem from the natural tendencies of human beings, and may even be sincere, even though misdirected efforts, of sisters to love truly. But faults and sins of uncharitableness are contrary to the very nature of human beings who were made by God to love. Just as surely as love is the essence of God and heaven, so is hatred the stuff of the devil and hell.

Most of the time, sisters do not accept the seriousness of these indulgences in various forms of hate and prejudice. They underestimate their moral responsibility to avoid them and tend to view them as part of the "natural" expectation of women. This is not true. Sisters are less than women when they transgress charity in these ways. Such sisters do not see the discrepancy between officially and publicly dedicating themselves to love and then living a life of habitual cold solitude and even of hatred in the convent. Through careful rationalization, they have become immunized to the damage done to others by the acid stings of these vices. They refuse to acknowledge not only that it is more injurious to rob a person of his reputation or his peace than to steal his material possessions, but that it also carries an even greater obligation of restitution. These violations of charity and justice are destructive of community spirit and of the works of the apostolate. In fact, sins against charity of which sisters make themselves guilty are the greatest obstacles to the cause of Christian love in the apostolate today.

This affiliation of uncharitableness may branch into a clique of several people. Such a group, motivated by antagonisms and aversions, can make conventual community life almost unbearable for those who will not succumb to their dictates. Sometimes sisters who are not loving project their unhappiness to their environment by joining others who suffer from similar cantankerous dispositions. Often, other sisters, well-meaning but weak, are drawn into these cliques because they are afraid to contradict the leaders. They know that loyalty is unknown to those who habitually criticize, and so they dread to become the object of the invectives they hear so glibly hurled at others. Indeed, scandal and disruption in the community are more often the results of these habitual and open violations of charity than of any other type of failure. The greatest sins committed in religious life are those against charity. Often, sisters who have developed these habits are guilty of the most serious form of "particular friendship."

It can happen through human weakness that sisters, even mature sisters, fall into some form of disordered living. In most cases these mistakes are not motivated by malice. Whatever the cause of their deviations, therefore, they will be humiliated rather than satisfied by their indulgences. Sisters who are mature will be able to face the reality of their errors honestly and do something constructive about them.

Other sisters may need help in assessing them correctly. First of all, they may need the benefits of the sacrament of penance. Often sisters are afraid to tell these facts to the confessor or to ask his advice about a situation if they are in doubt. They feel humiliated, especially if they think they must make detailed accounts. A confessor usually understands without the details. If a person says that she was dishonest in flattering another person and "using" her affection for selfish purposes, or that she touched her body to stimulate sexual pleasure, or that she calumniated a companion sister because she is jealous of her, or that she habitually criticized and opposed the superior and injured her reputation, the confessor will understand without details. If he needs more information, he will ask for it.

Sometimes sisters feel so ashamed that they hesitate to tell the truth in confession. This can be a subtle form of delusion or of rationalization for a sister. For instance, if a sister tells the confessor that she experienced sexual reactions during her sleep, but does not tell him that she was moody and constantly entertained sexual phantasies during the day, she is not giving him the total picture. Or if she asks the confessor if it is all right for a sister to kiss a student, but does not tell him that she is actively engaged in a sensual infatuation with the student, she is not being honest.

Another sister may confess that she was uncharitable to a companion sister several times. But the truth is that she entertains and nurtures a strong aversion for that sister because she is jealous of her, and this aversion prompts the unkind actions. Or she may acknowledge having judged another person rashly when the truth includes the fact that she expressed her judgment to others so that a person's reputation was harmed. In any of these instances, a sister is not being truthful with the confessor and really is jeopardizing her spiritual security.

It is earnestly hoped that priests who are confessors to sisters will be given more particular knowledge of the psychology of human funtioning, and that they will come to a more specific understanding of the psychology of woman, particularly the religious woman. Too often a priest is not able to help a sister with her problems simply because he does not understand her reactions as a woman or the nature of conventual community life.

Sisters who are not mature may need more help in redirecting their lives. In any event, sisters involved in this way should understand what is happening to them and why. Usually it is helpful if they can discuss the situations frankly and assist each other. If they are unable to do this entirely by themselves, a superior, another sister, or a confessor may assist them through counseling. In this way, they will renew and re-vitalize their love-relationship with Christ, and may even bring the disordered affection and inter-personal relations into focus, so that genuine love and kindness may result. They will need the strength of prayer, particularly the Mass and meditation. Then they must exert the self-discipline involved in forming new habits of living. In dealing with sisters, it is important always to treat them maturely and trustingly, helping them to understand the situation and to face it realistically.

If these sisters are taught how to love, they will then begin

to implement the more mature signs of affection: appreciation, loyalty, understanding, good fellowship, and a womanly
consideration for the feelings and rights of others. Those
sisters who do not know how to love must be given in-
structions about the meaning and dynamics of genuine love
in conventual living. Above all, they must be loved by
their fellow sisters.

Under no circumstances should a sister be treated coldly
or be made to suffer the effects of her mistakes through her
lifetime. It can be a crushing tragedy for a sister to be
"marked" forever because she has erred in loving. She should
be supported warmly with the same type of understanding
and sympathy which Christ gave so generously to those who
made mistakes. She should be completely accepted, loved,
and trusted without ever being reminded! Total forgiveness
always includes forgetting! This is Christ's prescription for
therapeutic TLC!*

* Tender, Loving Care.

Personal
Commitment

Personal Witnessing of Christ

People today are searching for the substantial and the genuine—the real in life. They are adept in recognizing it in a sister with integrity, and equally skillful in uncovering the mask of the woman who is really not living up to her religious vocation. They are perceptive in seeing through sham and will have none of the verbal philosophy of Christian love preached or written by a sister if she herself does not deem it important or acceptable enough to live it enthusiastically.

The image of contemporary religious life is like a mosaic. It is a composite of impressions and conclusions derived by lay people from the evidence expressed through the words and actions of sisters. (Let no one be deluded into thinking that sisters are not astutely observed and evaluated by the laity!) What a sister *is*—how she loves or does not love—is so constantly evident to those with whom she works in the apostolate, that often they don't even hear what she says she is or ought to be.

The sister who functions most effectively as an apostle is a mature person, possessed of the fullness of her womanhood. Christian love, translated into terms of practical daily living, is the keynote of her life and permeates all she is and all she does. The mature sister is real—she is herself—because she loves. Living love is the only way a sister can develop her individuality in self-realization. All pretense and imitation which make for self-consciousness and artificiality are eliminated in her. She really is what she seems to be and what she is supposed to be—a human apostle of love. The sister in contemporary society is wholesomely dignified because she respects herself and others. Likewise, she is completely unsophisticated because she is secure in her knowledge of the things that really matter to her. Indeed, she bears the marks of a truly cultured, gracious woman.

Whether she wills it or not, or whether she is aware of it or not, each sister makes either a positive or negative contribution to the cause of Christian love by her pattern of daily living. Even though she never makes a newsworthy public contact, her daily living becomes significant because every aspect of it reverberates through the life of the Mystical Body, strengthening or weakening it in some way, according to the Christian vitality of her love.

The life of a sister is an unceasing dialogue through which she constantly gives witness *to* Christ—or *against* Him. Her actions convey her attitudes much more aptly than her words. Usually it is not too difficult to give Christian love to others in major catastrophies or in circumstances of public significance, such as risking one's life to save children from a burning orphanage, nursing tornado victims in improvised hospitals, visiting people in slum tenements, or keeping night vigil at the deathbed of a Reverend Mother. But a sister's personal concern for people is really tested by her alertness in continually utilizing the dozens of ordinary means of showing love which are available in every day living. She is gentle in responding to the cantankerous demands of a terminal cancer patient who suffers a debilitating depression, or sympathetic in making inquiry about the neighbor's crippled child. Likewise, a sister can prove that she is really committed to the cause of love through such everyday occurences as graciously responding to a colleague's request for a favor, showing patient understanding for the needs of a mischievous student, manifesting love to companion sisters by constant cheerfulness, or by the genuine loyalty of making all persons feel "safe".

Further, the witnessing of Christ through love challenges a sister daily. The sister who is always courteous to her students need not take time to teach formal courtesy. On the other hand, if she is not respectful to them, all instruction in courtesy will be useless. Likewise, the sister who embarrasses a child before the entire class with sarcastic comments about his unpaid book bill need not waste time teaching him about kindness to others or consideration for their feelings. The sister who has profuse and public expressions of gratitude for the gifts from the lawyer's daughter (because her parents donate generously to the community building fund!), but coldly receives the homemade valentine from the child of a broken home, has taught the only lesson on Christian love which students will learn from her.

People somehow expect that a sister who publicly proclaims, through the wearing of a religious habit, that she is in love with Christ, should actually be producing evidence of this in her life. Her competent performance of duty and the practical personification of love in her life are so powerful that daily the world is better—or more disillusioned—because she is here.

Toward a Christian Philosophy of Life

The mature sister in the contemporary world needs a generous amount of balance. This equanimity presupposes values which are substantial and for which she is willing to organize her activities in a rational way. The way a sister lives is determined by what she believes about God, people, life, and eternity. If a sister is firmly convinced that life is a preparation for Heaven, which is an eternity of love, she has no logical alternative but to conclude that she must live the love of her vocation. She should be constantly aiming to solidify her identification with Christ by discerning what He expects of her. Therefore, she must spell out in detail her apostolic commitment of Christian love by becoming truly other-oriented as He is.

She must establish goals for herself which are human and realistic in current society, and which are within the spirit of community rule as well as the mind of the Church relative to religious life. She must understand well the specifics of her objectives. Hyper-generalized resolves "to be a good religious," "to do God's work," "always to do the most perfect action," or "to save souls" have no practical meaning and lose their efficacy in vagueness. Rather, she must determine such particular procedures as "to think optimistically," "to look for the good in people," "to praise the accomplishments of others," "to love others openly and warmly," and "to trust people by giving them the benefit of the doubt." Besides such well-formed, personalized, and attainable goals, a sister also needs the understanding and vitality necessary to integrate theory and practice in her life.

This whole directional set-up must, of necessity, be dominated by Christian love. Oftentimes, as St. Francis de Sales said, a sister makes a mistake by trying so hard to be an angel that she forgets to be a good human being. A sister must face the reality of herself and her environment, confident that, contacted wisely in cooperation with grace, all people and circumstances of life are potential channels through which she can come closer to God and share this privilege with others. She keeps her aims, accomplishments, satisfactions and all they mean in focus with Christ. And, if ever, through human weakness, she deviates from this alignment with Christ, she has the knowledge and the courage to re-charter her course of action. She devotes much prayerful thought and meditation to making this concrete philosophy an operational part of her life.

A sister must be aware that it is possible for her to verbalize an excellent philosophy of life without actually living it. In other words, there can be a gap between theory and practice in her living. A sister can piously attend every Mass in the parish church on Sunday morning, and refuse to speak to a student in her class all week. She can be perfectly conscientious in keeping rules of conventual silence, and, at the same time, constantly criticize the actions of a fellow sister. She can penalize a child for failing to prepare his homework without giving him a chance to explain, and respond with a temper tantrum to a fraternal suggestion which she feels is inappropriate. She can regiment students in a classroom through mechanical disciplinary procedures and chafe under the ordinary conventual daily schedule. She can speak with eclat' about the newest surgical procedure at a consultation with staff doctors, but treat the surgical patient with cold professionalism. In any of these situations, the sister has no real convictions about loving God and people. She does not love even though she may speak of it often and be capable of quoting scriptures *verbatim*. Such inconsistencies in living create tension in a sister and reduce her power for doing good to others.

Mature Acceptance of Reality

The mature sister is able to assess the reality of herself and her environment with reasonable accuracy and objectivity. She must take a penetrating look at herself and the circumstances in which she lives. This takes a rather unusual degree of honesty, a virtue, by the way, for which a sister should earnestly entreat God every day and spare no efforts to acquire. If a sister is to see life as it is, and not as she hopes it could be or as it ought to be—if she is to live in a real, and not a make-believe world—she must be able to make an objective appraisal of herself and her life.

The modern sister apostle respects the dignity of the unique, individualized human potential God gave her, and acknowledges the privileges of sharing the supernatural life of God through Baptism. She accepts the duties and joys of consecrated apostolic dedication in religious life as a means of realizing the spiritual maturity to which she is bound through the sacrament of Confirmation. She sees her religious vocation as a continuing renewal of her corporate unity with Christ, and of her function as His ambassador to the whole world. As a confirmed Christian, she stands daily in line to receive the apostolic commission of Christ Himself when He said: "You will receive the power of the Holy Spirit coming upon you, and you will be my witnesses. . . . to the very ends of the earth." (Acts 1:8) She values the human potential she has received from God as His personalized gift to her, as His way of showing His special individual love. This acceptance of herself as a person is also part of the humility essential to accepting and loving others. The mature sister esteems her humanness. She rejects as unchristian all puritanical proposals to crush human nature. In contrast, she deliberately proceeds to study it, to understand and to appreciate it, to accept and love it, to develop and control it within the framework of her religious vocation.

As a human being, a sister knows that she is equipped with a nature which has many qualities in common with other human beings, but which, in many ways, has a special individuality which is typically her own. Each person has many strong personality qualities. For instance, a sister may be naturally kind, generous, cheerful, reliable, and be consistent in practicing these virtues with considerable facility.

In addition, each person is also limited by certain shortcomings—traits which are not so good, but which she can change. For example, a sister may be naturally impatient and sensitive. Ordinarily, these traits are referred to as faults, but here they will be called challenges. No sister wants a fault because the implications, connotations, and denotations of faults in traditional religious life have become so negatively toned that sisters are threatened by them.

A sister may be dominated by the false notion that perfection automatically comes with a religious vocation. Or she may see personal perfection as a pre-requisite for, rather than a goal of Christian love in religious life. She may believe that she must eradicate everything human from her life in order to be a good sister, and she may attempt to do this by pretending the human does not exist. This will be true especially with regard to her faults. In many cases, this threat in accepting her humanness is so great that a sister will not admit her faults either to herself or to anyone else, and she will suffer the consequences in the form of emotional disturbance and an immature personality.

But challenges are different. Challenges tend to stimulate one to activity. If the sister who is impatient and sensitive by nature, sees these traits as challenges, she will make deliberate efforts to understand them and herself. "When am I impatient and sensitive?," "What causes these reactions in me?," "How do I manifest them externally?," "What would Christ do under these circumstances?," "What precisely can I do to improve?" Through honest answers and persevering efforts she gradually learns to be less sensitive. Instead, she becomes more reasonable in her evaluation of situations and her reactions to them. She does not allow herself to act impatiently but controls her impulses intelligently. This is a mature way of acting, the honest acceptance of an emotional reaction, and its regulation by principles of Christian love.

If a sister sees her undesirable impulses as challenges, she will use them as opportunities to show her love for Christ by making efforts to develop a mature personality, which will also facilitate her interaction with others. Thus she will become a better instrument of love. She will also recognize and improve her good characteristics, always according to her model—Christ. In this way, she will become as truly and magnificently human as God intends her to be. She will be genuine, without pretense, affectation or clumsy self-consciousness.

A sister owes this self-development to herself and to the people with whom she works. It will make it possible for her to understand, and to accept the challenges she sees in other people. She will be able to regard them positively, and, because she understands, she will not so readily become irritated by them.

Developing A Personal Love of Christ

If the sister in the modern world is to live the love that is her vocation, she must realize that she, as an apostle, draws her strength from personal closeness to Christ. Therefore, she must learn to know Him personally through prayer and an intensive, practical study of His life as presented in the New Testament. He must be real to her as a person, and she must know that she is special to Him.

This love relationship must, in the first place, be kept vital through prayer and the sacraments. There must be a conscious reality of the presence of Christ in her life. She prays—really communicates with Him on an intimate basis— because she knows and loves Him as a person. This is much more than just "saying prayers" to satisfy the requirements of prescribed spiritual exercises. Prayer can become too compartmentalized; that is, a sister may feel she has satisfied her "obligation" of prayer when she has attended conventual prayer sessions. She must understand that community prayer draws its efficacy from the communion of hearts of sisters, not from the communal recitation of oral prayers.

If a sister is to acquire the spirit of prayer, she should avoid the artificial repetition of ejaculatory prayers or compulsive attendance at chain novenas and holy hours. In these she may become a type of spiritual banker, counting ejaculations and indulgences as a measure of her closeness to Christ! Love knows no mathematical precision! It does not count its merits, bargain for rewards, nor restrict its prodigality!

For a sister apostle, prayer is never routine. Prayer does not mean physical presence plus the recitation of words and/or observation of rubrics. It is, rather, a real giving of self in a personal contact with Christ. She believes, without a doubt because He said so, that her love for Him is measured most significantly by her love of people. Therefore, she lives according to this belief. She knows that the kind of love she gives to others is perhaps the best indication of the quality of her communication with Christ in prayer. She knows how to bring Christ with her beyond the chapel door and to find Him in the people she meets. Everyone will know by the way she loves that she believes in Him and recognizes Him when she sees Him. The sister who does not, or will not love, has not yet really met God, and can never meet Him until she loves people. She can relate to God only as deeply as she can relate to people.

The sister apostle regards the Mass as her key opportunity for daily growth in love. With the present liturgical renewal, the essentials of the Mass have been set in focus and can be more easily understood as the source of the Christian activity of love. It is the communal Christian participation in the death and resurrection of Christ—the great act of salvation.

In the Offertory, the sister offers herself on the paten with the unconsecrated host to be transformed later into His likeness. Figuratively, she places there all her work, and her contacts with people, so that they, too, may all become Christ. As she adores Christ at the Elevation of the Mass, she realizes that she, too, is held up for all people to see—as she radiates love to them. They expect to see Christ in her. She must become like Him in her attitudes, reactions, thoughts, deeds, and words. She must be interested in His concerns. This they expect of her, because this is the activity to which she has formally and legally committed herself through her vows. In the Communion of the Mass, the supreme encounter with Christ, she has that intimacy of participation through which she will be transformed for the heroism of love to which she is committed.

During the day, she must find Christ where He is. He is in the people she meets and in the actual circumstances of her apostolic work. He is in her opportunities and in her obligations. He is also, less well seen, in the lack of these and in many of her failures. He is in those who help her and in those who hinder. He is even—and here surely against His will—in the evil machinations of others against her. In all of these contacts with Him, her life becomes a continuous renewal of the redeeming activity of the Mass.

The praying of the Divine Office is a formal opportunity for her periodically each day to re-emphasize and to strengthen this renewal of the Mass in her life. It is possible for a sister to become self-centered even in prayer by directing her considerations to selfish interests and needs. But, through the Divine Office, the liturgical prayer of the Church, she develops a Christian community awareness in uniting her supplications with those of all members of the Mystical Body.

The Divine Office, therefore, becomes the official framework of enlarged contact with God through which the objects and ends of her prayers are extended to include all those of the Church. She is no longer restricted by her narrowed scope of action, but learns from the social nature of the Office to worship God in a particular way by sharing the joys, sorrows, anxieties, and gratitude of the whole Christian world. Through the prayers of the Office, she reunites herself intimately with Christ, and sustains meaningfully the adoration, thanksgiving, reparation, and petition which began in the Mass. In appealing to God in the Office, a sister is not only an individual, but a functioning member of a corporate Church and thereby approximates the keen perception and universal commission of Christ Himself. Thus identified with Christ, she finds that the spirit of the Office influences her practical daily needs, mirrors her confidence, expresses her pleas, reflects her gratitude, sings her joy, comforts her sorrows, strengthens her resolutions, confirms her beliefs, proclaims her worship, and intensifies her love.

In mental prayer a sister contacts Christ intimately, visualizing the opportunities for living Christian love during the day, as He would have her accomplish it. She prays for the strength to carry it over into her daily living. A sister should often acknowledge the goodness of God by counting her blessings, and sincerely thanking Him for His gifts and help. Cognizance of God's personal love for her and His continuing assistance through the Holy Spirit, should be encouragement to strive continually for her Christian goal. Presuming adequate efforts and cooperation with God's grace, the mature sister can reasonably anticipate that she will succeed in loving well most of the time.

On occasion, in spite of sincere attempts, she may fail to achieve the objectives she has set for herself in practicing love. When this happens, she humbly approaches Christ, tells Him about it, re-evaluates the situation, renews her determination to love, and begins immediately to try again. Discouragement is a lack of trust in God and results from a failure to appraise situations honestly. Passing feelings of discouragement can be expected, but habitual states of depression should find no place in the life of a sister who loves.

A sister alerts herself to her goal and assesses her performance periodically. This gives her vision—the fruit of love— by which she has a perceptive awareness of reality as it is, and the honesty to accept and work with it realistically.

The examen should be an occasion for honesty with herself and Christ rather than a period of punitive self-depreciation. It becomes an opportunity for a sister to take positive inventory of her life, adoring, praising, thanking Christ, and asking for insight to see things as they are and for the courage to act upon them. The examen may be a brief form of the more lengthy considerations which have been made at meditation time. A sister looks squarely at herself and situations and call things by their right names. Dishonesty is deceitful, even when a sister does it. A lie is as much a falsehood for a sister as for anyone else. Injustice is as unfair when done by a sister as by a lay person.

It is important that a sister examine the reasons for her actions: "I told a lie because I was too proud to take the blame for something"; "I was impatient and curt with another person because I am jealous of her"; "I was dishonest because I am vain and unwilling to give credit to the one deserving it"; "I flattered another person because of fear of incurring displeasure or to procure a favor"; "I showed coldness because of a personal aversion".

These are meaningful evaluations in forming decisions toward a new approach to Christian loving. Such bald personal exposures make precise springboards to a more prolific apostolic love. In gratitude for the blessings and help God has given and in sorrow for the mistakes that have been made, a sister asks for help, knowing her complete dependence on God. This inspires a new course of action, a fighting determination to move ahead, because she loves Him and people. And on the days when she feels lethargic, she offers that to Him too, knowing that these human feelings need not touch the value of her love for Him or the vitality of her Christian loving.

The Way to Rational Living

The mature sister expects to have problems and frustrations because she understands that they are part of human living. She faces them as a mature woman—honestly, squarely, and promptly. To handle her problems realistically, she needs first to evaluate any situation as it is, and to be as objective as possible in collecting the facts: "What really happened?"; "What are my reactions?"; "What motivates my reactions?"; "How do others feel about it?" "What could I have done to improve or to avoid the situation?".

This is simply an enumeration of facts, not an outline of interpretations. The sister is not in a position to judge the motivation of others, but only that of her own actions. She must be cognizant of the influence of subjectivity in making these self-evaluations, and restrict herself to actual facts. She must discipline her imagination since she may, through self-pity, shame, or stubbornness be tempted to arrange or to create facts to make the situation more comfortable or convenient for herself. Such fictitious accounts blur reality and initiate trouble for her.

Then she refers them to Christ: "What does He think of it?"; "How would He react under these circumstances?"; "What must I do to love like He does?". She meditates on Christ's manner of loving people and of interacting with them, and compares her performance with His. In the light of all these considerations, she makes decisions and charts a prudent, rational course of action, which is possible in her particular situation. Finally, she acts on the decisions she has made and accepts the consequences of her choices. Facility in the process of rational acting is gained through practice, and this facility hastens the process.

The process of rational action may require that a direct attack be made on the situation, as would be necessary if a sister teacher were asked, for the first time, to teach modern

math to eighth grade students. Instead of collapsing psychologically and refusing to accept this assignment on the grounds
that, since she has never done it before she is incompetent
for the job, she sets about to study the techniques of the
math program in junior high school. Besides, she uses any
other help available to her, and conscientiously supplements
this initial orientation with daily preparation for each lesson
throughout the school year.

Or a sister can use her imagination in exploring new possibilities for handling a problem. This approach would be
needed if she were chairman of the committee of civic,
church, and professional people appointed to investigate the
drug problem as it affects teenagers of the local suburban
area in which she teaches. Research would be necessary to establish the specific picture of the *status quo* of the situation.
This sister would assume the leadership for the imaginative
thinking and constructive planning necessary to educate these
young people to more reasoned living.

Likewise, a sister may find it necessary to exploit some of
her personal capabilities, perhaps, as yet unchallenged, in a
new learning situation. Suppose a sister teacher is suddenly
incapacitated with a stroke. After weeks of hospitalization,
she has responded only partially to physical therapy. It is
evident that she will be unable to resume her teaching
duties. This can be a crushing blow for a sister, especially
if she feels unprepared for any other work. But if this sister
handles this difficult reality of her life well, she will come to
accept the inevitability of learning a constructive activity
which is possible for her in her present condition of health.
She will, for instance, be willing to learn sewing so she can

participate in the apostolate of her Community by contributing her services daily in the Community sewing room. The substitution of this new activity may never really satisfy her or take the place of teaching in her life, but she will find peace in accomplishing what she is able to do.

It is possible that a decision made in a rational way is at variance with that of a superior or contrary to the common good. For example, a sister principal of an elementary school and her faculty are convinced that it is educationally best to group children homogeneously according to learning ability and achievement level. So, on that basis, it is decided to assign third grade children in the school to three classrooms. The supervisor of elementary education does not share this policy of grouping children. After discussion of the assets of both homogeneous and heterogeneous grouping, she directs the sister principal to re-assign the classes in the third grade according to heterogeneous division. The sister principal must now conform to the directions of the supervisor since she has professional authority in this case, and the right to make the final decision. In conforming her actions to legal authority, the sister principal need not change her opinion about grouping children. She will, on the other hand, realize that there are pros and cons here which may make either opinion right. Therefore, she will see this, largely, as a matter of opinion, and not condemn the supervisor for acting in line with her particular point of view. She may be disappointed, but she will harbor no resentment. There need be no conflict here for the mature sister.

Through the personal discipline of a living faith and mature docility, religious and/or professional obedience is always reasonable and ennobling for her. She understands that if she is to practice religious obedience at all, she must think, form judgments, make decisions of her own, and then accept the decision of a superior even when it does not agree with hers. In action, she follows the direction of the one who has the responsibility of making the final decision in any particular event. However, if a sister is to escape the deadly inanities of "yes-people," it is important that she make decisions. She must "take a stand" in forming opinions about herself, people, and circumstances in life. She must evaluate the results of her decisions as unselfishly as possible, and then courageously accept the consequences which may result.

A sister forms her philosophy of life and assumes the responsibility for living it by making decisions in the light of rational convictions, even though she may not be in a position to execute them in all instances. This habitual decisiveness is precisely what makes her free to be herself, and gives her the liberty to choose the qualities which make her real. If she is to be real, she must know what she thinks, why she thinks it in every situation with which she is concerned, and consistently live according to her convictions. Since she has the courage and the freedom to live according to her convictions, her conduct is predictable. To live habitually in this rational way within the limits of the evangelical counsels and conventual rules is difficult for human nature, but it is the only way a sister can establish genuine equilibrium in her life. Through this wholesome independence, she preserves her integrity as a person, and is at peace with herself.

Even though in the name of religious obedience superiors

make assignments to particular activities and provide opportunities for development, a sister herself makes the major decisions in her life. Reverend Mother may ask a sister to teach fourth grade in Harvard Junction. But sister not only decides such crucial personal and apostolic issues as to know Christ and love Him as a person, to put vitality into her prayer life, to use every opportunity for professional advancement, to love people genuinely and humanly and to discover real meaning in her apostolic vocation, but she also determines the performance level at which she implements these decisions. She can, in large part, control such aspects of her life as the authenticity of her love for Christ, the caliber of her morning meditations, the excellence of her teaching and the effectiveness of her apostolic love. No amount of wishful thinking or provident arranging on the part of superiors alone can produce these blessings for a sister. She must want them enough to make herself responsible for getting them.

The restlessness which is evident in some sisters today does not stem so much from the pressures of contemporary conventual and apostolic living as from failure to assume the personal responsibility to align their daily living with the principles of Christ so they can develop personal peace.

The Necessity for Personal Discipline

To love consistently at a rational level within the spirit of the Christian commitment in religious life is not an easy task. It must be supplemented and sustained by intelligent personal discipline. A mature sister loves Christ personally and in her efforts to become like Him responds spontaneously to His love. Mortification is a means, not an end, in this process of becoming holy. Self-denial is never the weakness of stubborn endurance or of stoic repressions. It is, rather, the strength of regulative activity which, if kept moderated, purposeful, and constant, makes for intelligent self-government.

A sister should incorporate practices of self-denial and mortification into her daily activities in a natural, unassuming manner. Compulsion, fear, over-strain, or apprehension should be avoided in mortification. Edification is not a primary objective of mortification, but may be an accidental result. A mature sister is natural in her self-denial, and realizes that, for the most part, externally, it will go unnoticed and unappreciated by everyone but God. And this is as it should be. Self-discipline is one of the secrets of love between a sister and Christ as she endeavors to live more closely with Him. However, the over-all, indirect effects of well-ordered self-discipline will be observable in the degree of genuine holiness acquired by a sister. So often a sister surrounds the practice of self-denial with so much formality and contradiction that it is ineffective. She may set up such an artificial system of penance that it becomes a matter of ostentation with little relation to her daily life. For instance, she will not eat candy for a year or on a certain day of each week, or she will abstain completely from sugar or butter during Lent, or she will sleep without a pillow at night, or always avoid TV, or kneel without support during the litanies at night prayer. At the same time she is consistently impatient and curt with companion sisters, or lives in a constant state of moodiness, or is unreliable in preparing for professional work, or is cynical and caustic in judging others.

Balance must be established in this aspect of mature Christian living. Rightly motivated, acts of physical self-denial are good in themselves, but must also be supported by those of a psychological nature which touch the actual needs of the individual person. It is easy to be deluded about oneself and complacently to justify the choice of pious and unrelated mortifications which serve no other function than to formalize a code of self-discipline. A sister needs to choose the specific acts of self-denial which are necessary for her to become a better human being. Self-discipline is essential to prudential living and consequent peace and joy. A sister finds the best practices of self-denial in mature living of Christian love. She needs great faith to accept the inevitabilities of life with equanimity and to see them as the particular mortifications permitted her personally by God Himself. She can grow rapidly in Christ-likeness through the countless acts of self-discipline which present themselves daily, such as, smiling when she feels moody, listening open-mindedly to an opposing point of view, giving a person the judicial benefit of the doubt even when the evidence is marginal, controlling a habitually explosive temper, constructively facing the reality of the challenge of jealousy or insincerity, defending a person who is calumniated, telling the truth even when it is embarrassing, being interested in the needs of another even when fatigued. Such acts as these require heroic self-control and are leaven in substantial development of the Christian personality. There is even the possibility that a sister may need to eat candy every day, to sit during the litanies, and sometimes to enjoy two desserts instead of none at all, if she is to marshall enough physical strength to perform the more virile and purposeful acts of mortification.

Mortification includes the idea of penance which implies the need for reparation for sin. Genuine love seeks always to make up for the hurt it has caused, so the bold offenses offered to God so frequently through sin can be repaired through the love which prompts self-denial. A sister also knows that well-ordered penance helps to build up immunity to sin and to vitalize psychological and spiritual forces.

The Quest for Personal Maturity

A certain determination and assurance characterize the effective sister in the modern world. She knows who she is, where she came from, where she is going, and how to get there—and proceeds vigorously and happily to accomplish it. This gives her a stabilizing security. She can make reasonable decisions and readily implement them even though the inevitable consequences may not be naturally attractive to her. She is not easily daunted by difficulties because she has learned to trust implicitly in God, to appreciate and accept His constant providential affection for her, and to return it in full measure. She trusts people. She has great confidence in the capability of human beings, including herself, to change for the best. She has the prudence necessary to exert responsible influence in changing the environment when she can, and the courage and patience to accept it when she cannot. She suffers intelligently by accepting pain as part of her life. Because she knows how to love, she is able to bear pain with resilience so that it enriches, rather than crushes her. She learns wisdom from life's frustrations and reverses, and is always better, never bitter, because of them.

The sister who becomes bitter fails to see purpose in her heartaches. It is true that on occasion human business can seem so devoid of both rhyme and reason that, apparently, it not only violates all laws of common sense, but also those of justice and charity as well. A sister can be hurt deeply by people and circumstances in life. Sometimes when adversities and complications of life touch her to the depths of her being, it may be almost humanly impossible for her to endure them without experiencing varied mixtures of hurt, anger, resentment, disappointment, and discouragement. That she has feelings of bitterness is human. These feelings are damaging only when a sister allows them to touch her real self and to determine the pattern of her living. Then the beauty of life for her is diminished, if not destroyed, by a withering cynicism, which soon becomes habitual. Her fervor as an apostle loses its verve and she gradually dies psychologically. It can be extremely difficult, under these circumstances, to keep surging emotional reactions in control so they do not clog the channels of rational thinking. Bitterness is most readily blasted by active faith and vigorous love through which a sister acknowledges that God has design in the suffering. Therefore, she can believe that He has a reason for permitting it, even though He may choose not to divulge it to her. Understanding pain does not lessen its poignancy, but gives a sister the tranquillity of spirit necessary to trust His love so she can reap maximum personal enrichment from it. The sister who really loves sees pain as the testing ground of her love, and meets the challenge by becoming a better person because of it.

Equanimity brings peace and composure to the contemporary sister. She has quiet and freedom in heart and mind. Peace comes with the patient acceptance of life as God supervises it for each individual Christian. Responsible acceptance is never either passivity or a "grit-your-teeth" type of endurance in painful or uncomfortable experiences of life; nor is it a shallow manifestation of pleasure when receiving life's blessings. Rather, it means the ability to realize the providential care of God for each person in the events of life, whether they are joyous or humanly difficult to take. It is the actualization of the gift of faith for which a sister needs the vision of Christian love, the insight born of closeness to Christ and of loving people, and the optimism to see good in the events of life clearly, to increase it, to emphasize it, and to use it vigorously in apostolic endeavors.

These fruits of genuine trust in God and others are essential to real apostolic living. They depend on a sister's directing and controlling her life according to the realization of Christ as an ever-present, personal reality in her life. The sister in the modern world lives in the space age—an age of speed and movement and change. Often the speed, movement, and change do not seem to have purpose or mature direction. The sister-apostle must take time to think, to pray, to contemplate, to organize, to love Christ and people purposefully even amidst the external bustle of environmental activity which is part of loving people. Things in a sister's life must be so ordered that her external poise is actually an indication of her well-ordered emotional state. This stability makes for sturdiness of purpose and perseverance, and eliminates vacillation and doubt. A sister may develop a Spartan hardiness in endurance so that an emotionally surging interior may be cloaked under an apparently calm exterior. This condition is unnatural and cannot be maintained for long. Disaster of some kind is bound to be the climax of such tension. Love cannot be fructified in this imbalance.

The sister in the modern world is every religious woman in every convent across the nation. Opportunity for personal commitment in Christian love is at her door. She need not wait for superiors to initiate spectacular changes in her Community in the name of modern adaptation. All concerns of the modern apostolate can be and should be influenced significantly by each religious woman who vitally lives the love of Christ that she has vowed. She must see this as her personal responsibility and realize what tremendous powers she has to influence the world, by *being* a real apostle of love; that is, the strong, but tender woman of God who relates to people so lovingly that the world is better because she is here. The truly holy sister who totally commits herself to love as a modern apostle knows that her maturity as a person and her competence as a Christian woman are always the greatest contributions she can make to any situation.

Apostolic
Relevance

Personal Involvement in The World

The nature of the Christian commitment—loving God above all things and her neighbor as herself—demands that a sister become involved physically, psychologically, and spiritually in the current circumstances of her apostolic environment. A sister endeavors, therefore, to understand the world in which she lives. She develops a rational, productive relevance to her surroundings, and becomes part of it as a leaven of God's love, through Christ-like kindness, understanding, sympathy, and service which she consistently gives to others.

In relating apostolically to the 20th century environment, a sister must not only be *in* the world, she must be *of* it. This holy relevance means that she must be a part of all she meets: absorbing heartaches so the burdens are easier to bear, sharing joys so happiness increases, supplying encouragement for strong living, giving silent testimony to a Father's forgiveness so sin can be repaired, and bringing knowledge and understanding to bear on prejudices which motivate inhumanities among men.

A mature sister is close to Christ and is not afraid of relating intimately with her environment. She is really free to love. She is not fearful of becoming worldly, because she knows that worldliness is not restricted to a particular way of life, or to a certain geographic area, but is found in thoughts, words, and deeds which oppose God and His law of charity. So while she is reasonably vigilant and prudently fearless in overcoming the viciousness of worldliness no matter where it is found, she is not fearful of God's world and the people He makes. She loves them wholeheartedly and lets them know it! The apostolate includes all God's people— those who know, love, and serve Him already, those who are still waiting to learn of Him, and those who reject Him. People in the apostolate are real human beings who are made of flesh and blood as well as of spirit. A sister must bring Christ to them in human ways which they can understand and appreciate. She must learn to know them, to love them, to influence them, to serve them—and not just to superimpose a Christian culture on them in an artificial, impersonal way.

Equipped with love and a deep sense of commitment, a sister must share the joys and difficulties of others as they are. Problems are normal to human living and are a part of life for all Christians, including sisters. But a sister must not just accept this fact coldly; she must make an effort to understand, to face the truth of life in all its ruggedness, with compassion. She must really salt the earth with the Christness that is in her. She must experience, at least vicariously through sympathy, the problems of lay people, if she wants to understand them, and really to share Christ with them. Sisters who have never been hungry without hope of getting food, or who need not worry about the monthly rent or last year's still unpaid doctor bill, or who have not endured the poverty of having "everything money can buy" as a substitute for parental affection, or who have not agonized in the desertion of a loved one, often become callously disinterested and unconcerned when these problems confront lay people. Sisters should take time and effort to relate in a real, understanding way with the actualities of life as experienced by their charges and co-workers. These are the channels of love—with the sisters as instruments—which God often uses in redeeming His people.

Too often the religious woman has unwittingly cut herself off from apostolic opportunities by a divisiveness resulting from a misinterpretation of the meaning of her role as a religious apostle in the Church. Sometimes a sister does not seem to understand that the Christian goal—loving God and people—is the same for all Christians regardless of the means they choose to accomplish it. In fulfilling the laws of love, Christians in the married or single lay state are bound only by the commandments, while a sister has freely assumed the added obligations of the counsels of consecrated chastity, obedience, and poverty.

It is important, however, that a sister remembers that she is first a Christian and therefore is also obligated primarily by the commandments. She must keep a correct order in this, so she understands that as a Religious, she is not automatically better than other Christians. All Christians, no matter what their particular way of life, become holy only to the degree that they exert personal efforts to LOVE —God and people. The means to this common goal are substantially the same for all Christians. A sister dare not construct barriers between herself and lay people by affecting attitudes of spiritual and moral superiority! She should consider that she does not have an option on sanctity since "all

Christians are saints by vocation." (St. Paul, Romans 1:1.) Militant Christian love is the yardstick of Christian holiness in any vocation, and the commission to live love is a mandatory assignment, not a fringe benefit of an arbitrary appointment.

Further, there are sisters who must battle the presumption that Christ's work is reserved for them alone; just as there are those who must be jolted out of the torpor that minimizes the responsibility for active apostolicity on the part of religious women. Heretofore, emergency and expedience usually set the tone for apostolic interaction with lay people. Since there were not enough sisters to fill the classrooms, the nursing positions, or the secretarial jobs, sisters accepted lay people as assistants in their work because they needed them. Or sisters were satisfied with a nominal and static Christian appearance of "keeping the conventual rule," leaving the militant evangelical membership in the Mystical Body to the laity.

A new and more honest perspective is in order. Sisters must realize that apostolic business will never be satisfactorily accomplished unless they cooperate with lay Christians. Merely working with lay people as contributing spectators or partial auxiliaries is not enough. Sisters must permit them really to become incorporated into the total operational apostolate. The shared contributions of lay people and sisters working together in unity are necessary to the Christian completeness of apostolic work. And even if there should ever be a utopian era in which there would be a sufficient number of sisters to do all the tasks of their assigned apostolates, the cooperation of lay people can never be honestly dispensed with if the work of the Church is to be whole.

Sisters should always choose to invite lay people to share their apostolic efforts. If concern for the apostolate is genuine, sisters and lay people must really link forces in witnessing Christ. It is true that some aspects of apostolic activity will be done best by each group individually, but much of the work of the Church can be done only through the corporate action of the laity and sisters working under the direction of their Bishops. Work in any apostolic area should be done by those persons who are most qualified in any particular situation. Therefore, if a lay person on a faculty is best prepared to be the principal in a parochial or a private school, he should have the position. Also, sisters must make frank admission that often lay people would perform better than sisters in certain apostolic functions, such as business administration or public relations tasks, and open-mindedly allow them to take the lead. The Christian teamwork involved here is much more than judicious or convenient tolerance. It means integral coaction and whole endorsement characteristic of real Christian love.

The Pursuit of Excellence

Enthusiasm, a part of apostolic relevance for the mature sister, is true zeal, a genuine spirit of dedication and wholehearted commitment. It is an externalization of sincere convictions of the worth of the cause. Only the sister who is informed about or prepared for her work can really have convictions about it. There must be preparedness, spiritually, psychologically, professionally. The sister in the modern world sees the aspects of her religious vocation—spiritual and professional—as mutually supporting in her efforts to become an apostolic saint. Young women contemplating the religious life today attach much importance to the type of developmental opportunities a Community provides for its members.

The day is gone when a religious woman will be accepted just because she is "one of the good sisters." She must be well-prepared for her task in the apostolate. She must aim for scholarship proper to her profession by developing her talents and exploiting her powers of creativity. Her capabilities are a sacred trust which within the framework of her religious life, she is obligated to cultivate and externalize in such a way that the cause of Christ is thereby furthered in a constructive manner. The sister in the modern world who is truly enthusiastic about her apostolate is creative and colorful in her performance of duty. She has vision, and not visions, so she wisely uses the material gifts of God and the technical inventions of man to radiate love in the apostolate. She finds God's cues in all His creation! She gets His messages through intelligent use of mass media of communication—TV, radio, cinema, the press—as certainly as in the solid spiritual reading of Chardin, Häring, and Suenens. She recognizes His heart beat in the rhythm of the Hootenanny's "Happy Wanderer" as readily as in the polyphony of a choir's "Panis Angelicus." She picks up His wave length in the stereophonic concert as surely as in the chant of her favorite litany. She appreciates Him in the automation of modern household appliances as well as in the new liturgical developments. She generates His joy at the

Community picnic with the same vivacity with which she radiates His love in teaching the Math class. She lives very close to God because she continually discovers Him everywhere and in everything!

Further, a sister must actually be capable of excellent performance in her field. She owes competence to those with whom she works. This is a matter of Christian justice. Vowed obedience gives a sister a new motivational impetus for any task, but it never gives her competence in her work. This implies that the individual sister has an obligation in conscience to seek and to use available opportunities for personal and professional development. In traditional religious life, some sisters have canonized the heresy that the more inhuman they could be and the less competent they could become, the holier they would be. In too many instances, this theory has been viewed by them as true humility, so they have used it as rationalization for their apathy. As a result, thousands of personal talents—gifts of God to sisters—have been dutifully buried in sterility under religious habits! Think of the Christian love that could be generated if this latent apostolic power were productively tapped and put to work for Christ!

A sister realizes, however, that in becoming highly specialized or skilled professionally, she must be genuinely educated as well as highly degreed. She must love! Love is the essence of true education. Love alone transforms academic scholarship, occupational competence, and personal attractiveness into prolific stimulants of apostolic action. The sophistication which can result when a sister selfishly sees opportunities for advancement as prestige privileges devastates the meaning of the Christian commitment of love.

When a sister enters religious life, she makes a tacit contract with her Community to devote herself with diligence to the profitable utilization of the opportunities which the Community, in turn, by virtue of the same contract, obligates itself to provide for her. A sister should take this responsibility seriously. Religious life is the only social institution which keeps its members even if they do not measure up to its standards. If a sister, for instance, were a lay teacher, she would be expected to keep abreast with all the curricular developments of her teaching field, and to adhere to the administrative policies and regulations of the school, as well as to abide by the norms of the profession in general. If she failed to do so, she would be asked to withdraw from the school system and to seek employment elsewhere. But in conventual life, a sister who deviates from prescribed requirements is not penalized in this manner. Sometimes a sister may be tempted to take advantage of the security of knowing that she will be maintained and supported by the Community in spite of the caliber of her contribution to the apostolate.

A sister needs to admit to herself that she has talents. God gave them to her. She must be convinced, also, that she should use them. He expects this of her. Occasionally, a sister may need to make known her abilities to her superiors. She cannot expect her superiors always to know her personal talents and professional aptitudes and preferences unless she informs them. This is done with the propriety of excellent communication which should exist between superiors and subordinates in religious life. The mature sister realizes that the ultimate decision for the disposition of her abilities rests with superiors, and therefore, is willing to accept it, even when it is contrary to her expectations. She understands that as a mature adult she is expected to exert responsible influence on circumstances in her life, but she knows, too, through faith and reason, that God often indicates His specific designs for her through her superiors under religious obedience. She should not, however, be discouraged if at first she meets apparent lack of interest or understanding on the part of her superiors. She should give them the benefit of the doubt by concluding that they are preoccupied with the concerns of their office, and courteously approach them soon again to re-state her suggestions and requests.

It is important for superiors to realize that often the Holy Spirit chooses to manifest His wisdom through sister subordinates in a religious community. So superiors, in turn, should give every sister a hearing, and reasonably provide circumstances which will allow her to utilize her talents effectively in the apostolate. This is Christian honesty on two scores: first, to the sister herself who is obligated to use her talents, and secondly, to those with whom she works who have a right to expect the best she has to give. This puts a responsibility on religious superiors to provide sound spiritual and psychological formation and adequate professional preparation for sisters. The new theological thinking constantly being evolved in the Church today and the multiple opportunities for educational scholarship and professional competence must be used to advantage in the formation and development of sisters.

It is evident that prudence is necessary in appraising personal talents, since it is possible that a sister may be deluded in thinking she possesses capabilities which she does not actually have. It is presupposed, further, that in the name of Christian truth, sisters will never be assigned to apostolic tasks for which they are not sufficiently prepared. The cause of Christian love in the apostolate can be irreparably damaged by such flagrant gestures of professional dishonesty as directing a sister without formal teacher education to a classroom because she "loves little children"; assigning a sister with a LPN certificate to take charge of the Radiology department of a hospital because she "always wanted to work with x-ray"; appointing an emotionally insecure sister to the superiorship because "she feels rejected and authority will make her feel accepted"; maintaining a sister in a task for which she is initially incompetent or for which her ability to function effectively has waned because "she will be hurt if she is transferred."

Unjust, too, are such instances of professional illogicality and extravagance as asking a sister with a master's degree in sociology to pursue advanced studies in hospital administration because "she is competent in managerial affairs and there is a hospital construction project in the offing"; sending the sister with the doctorate in political science, who has had fifteen years experience in teaching related subjects, to teach second grade "to keep her humble and the other sisters edified"; directing an excellently qualified eighth grade teacher who loves her work with teenagers to administer a secondary school because "in her current assignment she is too well liked by students and their parents." These are questionable negotiations which must be detrimental to the personal integrity of the sisters concerned and to matters of apostolic efficiency, even if they are sincerely transacted in the name of religious obedience.

These actions are psychologically criminal to the individuals concerned and to those with whom they work. Great harm is done to the apostolate through these unchristian approaches in utilizing personal talents in an apostolic way. Actually, such transactions, heavy with personal liabilities for sisters, are vestiges of the "plant-cabbages-upside-down" techniques of a medieval monasticism.

Often, a sister does not accept her current assignment in teaching, nursing, homemaking, social work, or whatever it may be, as her apostolic endeavor. Thus the teaching sister might regret that ordinarily she has no opportunity for "apostolic communication" though she teaches all week, and sees as "apostolic" only the hours of catechizing she does in a slum area on Saturday mornings. Religious women who thus segregate themselves from meaningful participation in the front line activity of the apostolate of their Community, convey these attitudes in word and action, so that people fail to see dedication in religious life as the apostolic endeavor it really is. It is no wonder, then, that students sometimes say, and rather casually at that, that they have decided not to enter a convent, but rather to work in the apostolate of the Church.

The specific activities in which a sister engages, whether it be teaching, nursing, or social work, are not of prime importance, however. The high quality of professional preparedness and the degree to which she identifies herself with Christ and transmits this Christ-likeness to others are the determining elements in her apostolic effectiveness. Genuine apostolic influence stems from a Christian love that is as warm as it is strong, as honest as it is loyal, and as free as it is enduring. Various kinds of surface charm of special-occasion philanthropy may masquerade as apostolic love, but eventually their superficiality is exposed by the rugged realities of human interaction.

If a sister cannot be Christ-like in her present occupation, how does she presume that she could be different if she merely changed her sphere of activity? Such superficial change will not automatically accomplish the necessary transformation. Perhaps some sisters who are college instructors should leave their rostrums and lead discussions in Newman Club meetings, or sisters who teach elementary school children should abandon the self-contained classrooms and teach in confraternity centers, or sister nurses should leave their modern surgical arenas and work in culturally deprived sections of metropolitan areas. These new tasks, however, like the old, will be fruitful only if the sister apostles, fortified with formal preparation for their new field of social service, really love Christ, and openly communicate Him to others through their work. But until Holy Mother Church, through the Bishops, directs higher superiors of religious communities to undertake new apostolic labors—and this may well be in the plans of God—sisters will fulfill their vocations by exerting efforts to use their current work as a witness stand for the love of Christ.

It is always necessary to examine rather carefully the motivation that underlies suggestions for change in apostolic activity on a community-wide basis. It is possible that, rather than prompted by eagerness to love better, some sisters see occupational adaptation as a release from current frustrations, or as a means to escape the apostolic obligations which have become meaningless for them. At the same time, religious superiors must ever be cognizant of their responsibility to cooperate with the Church in initiating profitable expansion of apostolic works for sisters. They should not take their traditional heritage for granted as the best answer for today's apostolic demands, without seriously investigating the meaning and value of more pertinent involvement. They will also be astute in re-structuring formation programs for the youngest members of their Communities. The developmental approach which was satisfactory years ago will, for the most part, no longer suffice. Young women aspiring to a life of dedication as religious apostles today must be taught a philosophy seasoned specifically for the needs of the current apostolate. Superiors should not be afraid to explore and to test new means of Christian living. They should encourage and permit their sisters to engage in the apostolic works being opened by the Church today.

Leveling The Barriers to Apostolic Love

The cause of Christ—apostolic love—must go forward with a momentum and rate of advancement comparable to that of the current ecumenical thinking in the Church. Our late Holy Father, the great Pope John XXIII, through his magnificent and warm-hearted love, set the pace for leveling the barriers to apostolic communication in the Christian world. Religious women of today, with the same objective in view, must follow this lead by making intelligent adaptations in conventual living.

Change, for its own sake, is usually inadvisable. Rules are not necessarily inadequate because they are old, and, on the other hand, neither are they sacrosanct because "it has always been done this way." Every change in conventual living deserves the name of true adaptation only when it has direct and specific bearing on the actual practice of Christian love.

Each sister should see adaptation, not as a means of providing an easy, luxurious, or comfortable life for herself, nor as a violation of the spirit of religious living, but as an opportunity to revitalize her religious vocation in loving and serving better in the apostolate. Changes in religious life are important and relevant only when they are judged in this perspective of Christian love.

Current demands in conventual life and professional activity cannot be satisfied with rules and regulations which were tailor-made for, and apropos to, a less demanding era. Adaptation implies changing conventual circumstances so apostolic living and loving will be facilitated for sisters as human beings. All circumstances in religious life should be examined and questioned for Christian meaning and purpose in the light of contemporary apostolic needs and requirements. Attention should be directed to the formation of new concepts and the re-defining of old ones in pertinent aspects of religious life. Perfectionism in the external details of religious life, for instance, cannot be equated with holiness, nor fear with prudence. Neither can regimentation be identified with order, nor uniformity with unity. Lethargy cannot pass for meekness, or passivity for humility. Legalism is not synonymous with religious obedience, nor righteousness with right. Such misconceptions have long confused the thinking of sisters. These ideas are due for a re-examination in the *aggiornamento* theme, so that every sister will know that love is not dehumanizing softness nor romantic bliss. Love is holiness—a virile, vital affection for God and people—the core of a sister's life.

She will know that freedom is not flagrant irresponsibility, but the liberty of spirit which disengages her from selfishness so she can love as Christ loved; that initiative is not rebellion, but the blessed ambition without which she cannot become a saint of love; and that peace and joy are not the fruits of pampered indulgence, but the rewards of an ordered and human living of Christian love.

Rules and customs in community living are not significant in themselves, but only as a means to holiness. Therefore, they should be starkly re-appraised according to the degree to which they specifically aid sisters in practicing Christian love in the apostolate.

Customs in religious life for sisters who participate in an active professional apostolate should have special dimensions. Ample allowance should be made for initiative in making adjustments to local circumstances. Often conventual practices are not only contradictory and inhuman, but also at great variance with ordinary Christian living, and out of harmony with prevailing cultural norms. Such practices can make sisters seem so odd, and religious life so outdated that possibilities for communication with fellow Christians are seriously curtailed. Religious life would be seen then, as a maze of irrelevancies, futilely detached in its smug isolationism from the reality of human Christian living. Apostolic communication between sisters and lay people may thus be made awkward and embarrassing or even be prohibited entirely.

Religious habits, when designed without reasonable consideration for fashion and utility, may be so formidable that they actually frighten people—or perhaps amuse them—and therefore, make them either reluctant to approach sisters or inclined to ridicule them. The problem of conventual attire is much more extensive than might, at first, be apparent to the casual observer. The reluctance on the part of some sisters to modernize their garb may indicate that probably they see habit changes of any nature as a challenge to the distinctive religious habit as such. Or their hesitance to alternate antiquated or impractical habit designs may come from fear of experimentation, unwillingness to break a dedicated adherence to tradition, or failure to examine objectively all possible alternatives in handling this question. But whatever the deterring factors may be, those concerned about or responsible for purposeful habit modifications for sisters must take a long look at all aspects of the major issues involved. Questions must be asked about sisters' habits. The correct answers may be as diverse as private opinion or as relative as the varying needs of different sisterhoods. But since ultimate solutions to the habit problem for sisters are waiting to be worked out, it may be pertinent to reflect on some practical angles of this current conventual need.

First of all, it seems contrary to Christian common sense

that sisters who take a vow of poverty should be compelled to wear unnecessary yards of expensive habit material because "it has always been done," instead of using moderate yardage in a contemporary and dignified style with the less costly synthetic fabrics currently available. Besides, as human beings, sisters could work more freely if clothing were adapted to climatic conditions, even on the home front. Sisters can be as holy—and surely much more comfortable—if they are permitted to wear habits of featherweight, drip-dry dacron in summer, (or any time of the year, for that matter) instead of the coarsely woven mohair habit so often prescribed by rule.

In general, undue importance has been attached by tradition to the attire of sisters. Unwittingly, a particular religious habit has become a conventual status symbol which has significance for sisters well beyond its merits. There always is the danger that a sister inadvertently considers her habit as her sanctification rather than as a sign of it. A sister is not a religious, an apostle of love, because she wears a habit, any more than she would be a nurse solely because she donned the white cap and uniform of a nurse. Complacent reliance on the merits of dress alone can prompt a sister to a lassitude by which she enjoys the benefits of religious life without paying the premiums of striving for real holiness.

Originally, the religious habit was merely the external identification of those women who chose to become saints by devoting all their talents and time to God and His people. Its simplicity and practicality attracted no spectacular attention, so it was not an obstacle to sisters in working with people. But the religious habit that once was unostentatious in blending with styles of the last century, now becomes obvious in bleak contrast to contemporary fashions, and may subtly impede the work of sisters.

Considerations of severe modifications of religious habits for sisters are in order. Several pertinent questions must first be answered. Can a religious habit, conspicuous because of antiquated style, really signify a Christian love that is completely contemporary? Would rigid simplification and modernization of religious habits influence the intrinsic value of apostolic work done now by sisters? Is it possible that the adoption of a common and distinctive uniform by sisters in all religious communities would be more indicative of ecumenical activity in the Church, and would, therefore, assist religious women to establish more meaningful unity in their particular apostolates? Besides, other practical matters demand the attention of those suggesting the adoption of completely contemporary styles for religious habits. Undoubtedly, this would be a much more complicated development than is immediately obvious to the uninitiated. Problems of appropriate grooming, pertinent to an effective apostolate, are bound to increase. First of all, there would be the important necessity of keeping in style. And such fashion details as hem lines, neck lines, and belt lines, for instance, have a way of fluctuating rather radically within a short period of time. Fashion-wise, it is a less noticeable violation of good taste to be out of style by one hundred years than by only two or three!

Further, consider a few related questions of convention, which not only may be observed rather critically by lay people, particularly by the modern aspirant to religious life, but may also be disturbing to a sister's sense of womanly propriety. Would the traditional black conventual oxford be a suitable accessory for a contemporary suit or dress? Would the same style of contemporary attire be proper for sisters of all ages? How essential is consideration for personal tastes and physical differences? Should middle-aged and older sisters be expected to wear patterns preferred by college-age novices and junior sisters? Would a religious habit in a contemporary style mean that sisters, of necessity, must spend the valuable time they would otherwise devote to apostolic efforts maintaining a wardrobe, making clothes with tailored precision, and styling their hair with modern rolling, teasing, or brushing devices? It will have to be determined whether such reflections about the religious habit, in any way, touch the essence of profitable adaptation for sisters.

Over and above all this, there is the realistic possibility that perhaps all the current emotional consternation and editorial furor about nuns' habits may be nothing more than aimless, even though presumably sincere, controversy about a fundamentally inconsequential issue! Recently, it seems that everyone—those who know and those who don't, those who are interested and those who couldn't care less, those who have power to effect reform and those who have no authority at all, those who are in the convent and those who are not, those who have always openly championed the liberal cause and those who have never before even bothered to form an opinion—all these suddenly feel qualified to speak dogmatically and conclusively about the matter of religious habits!

It could well be that habits worn by sisters do not significantly matter at all to anyone, if the sisters who wear them are real, honest-to-goodness persons. Perhaps, the grandmother who lives next door to the convent doesn't even see what the sister wears as long as she can appreciate the involvements of keeping African violets in bloom through a long, cold winter, or the art student who gets the sister teacher's approving smile doesn't care that her face is encased in highly starched Indianhead, or the long-term TB patient who feels the sustaining support of the sister nurse's understanding is unconcerned that her heart beats regularly under layers of pleated serge, or the tousel headed nine-year old orphan boy who learns a little more about love because sister can bat a ball that clears the bases isn't aware that she is plain-shod in the most prosaic of flat-heeled Red Cross models, or the man across the street doesn't really notice much observable difference (except the price!) between the sister's medieval coif stiffly piled on her head and his wife's latest floral headgear—imitation a la Dior!

Could it be that attention in the great discussion of adaptation should be diverted from such non-essentials as religious habits and rather be directed first to the salient aspects of sisters becoming real women—apostles who can witness Christian love so genuinely that it penetrates misplaced hemlines, unnecessary pleats, and extravagant yardage? It is much more difficult for sisters to be real persons than to design and to wear costumes which will make them look authentic when they are not! But since it is possible for sisters to be real people and at the same time to be appropriately and comfortably attired, let them open-mindedly make decisions about their practical needs, courageously make changes accordingly, and enthusiastically be about their business of living Christian love.

It can happen, too, that lay people are puzzled and sisters are shackled by the incongruity of conventual rules which, for example, permit a sister to have lunch with lay people in a university cafeteria during a professional convention, but which forbid her to enjoy a cup of coffee with family and friends in the convent parlor on visiting day. The spirit of religious living could not be damaged—and the human appeal of religious life surely would be increased— if such conventual legislations were aligned with the harmless American custom of socializing which usually includes some kind of refreshments. It is amazing what the aroma of a good cup of coffee can do to take the edge from human difficulties or to warm the good fellowship of friends! Sisters must be ingenious in converting all circumstances into channels of love. This is part of the Christian business of loving God and people!

There is often a rigidity in the behavior of sisters that seriously impedes smooth relationships with lay people. The stiffness of cold ritualism can make sisters seem like mannequins or automatons rather than real, human people with warm blood pulsing in their veins. Operative apostolic functioning can be obstructed by displays of regimentation, as for instance, when sisters proceed into the parish church for Sunday Mass with the formality of a military line-up. They walk two-by-two the full length of the middle aisle and sit comfortably with geometric exactness in the pews reserved for them in the front of the Church, while lay Catholics crowd uncomfortably into the remaining pews. Would it not be better for sisters to avoid this divisive formalism, and to go to church freely in small groups or individually, and sit next to their fellow Christians in any available places in the church? Such conventual regulations, which formerly may have had meaning, but which now are pretentious and/or artificial, complicate Christian interaction for sisters in the apostolate. It is necessary to change to practices that will more adequately serve the sisters in living the complete religious life.

Sisters in the modern apostolate are expected to engage in activities unknown to sisters twenty-five years ago, such as attending evening meetings and formal afternoon teas, traveling alone on occasion, doing their own shopping, supervising the community business negotiations of large construction projects, serving as consultants on advisory committees, functioning effectively in professional groups on an equal basis with lay colleagues, driving cars and traveling by plane, as well as constantly keeping pace with the academic and social demands of the active apostolate.

All this taxes the strength of sisters. Sisters cannot be expected to carry on their professional obligations and simultaneously engage in peripheral activities which could be done by hired assistants. Sisters who teach, for example, should not also be expected to bear the full burden of the secretarial tasks of teaching or of the housekeeping jobs involved in maintaining their convent homes. Major secretarial and maintenance projects should be done by hired help. This is a place where lay people can share the apostolate with sisters. Consideration of money, which usually is the major deterring factor here, is not a matter of poverty; it is, rather, a matter of charity to the sisters and to those with whom they work. Sisters should not be expected to spend long hours typing cumulative records, scrubbing floors, or washing walls after full time work in an apostolic field. Sisters are human—and no amount of love of God can make them withstand these pressures which overrate their very humanness! Thought should be given to the fact that while sister teachers, for instance, engage in these manual tasks, they are sacrificing the valuable time they should, in conscience, be giving to preparation for their apostolic work. Considered in this light, the ethics of such conventual situations become obviously questionable!

The lay people who are asked to assist sisters in this way should be remunerated in money or its equivalent. If current salary standards for religious women do not adequately meet the needs of contemporary apostolic living, appeal should be made to the proper authority for adjustments toward realistic living wages. This is a real problem for sisters. The cost of living and the expense involved in preparing sisters for a professional apostolate have steadily increased, while, in many instances, the monetary compensations given to sisters have deadlocked at a level that is almost operationally impossible.

Sisters, motivated by Christian love—the true spirit of religious life—should be free to participate in their apostolic obligations without countless regulatory stipulations which are neither important in themselves nor contributory to the practice of Christian love. It is unfair to sisters to grant permissions to them which are so heavily weighted with qualifying interpretations that the meaning of the original permission is negated for all practical purposes. This might occur, for instance, when permission is granted for a day of relaxation for the sisters. The real objective of such a permission is entirely lost when superiors, without consideration for preferences and tastes of individual sisters, direct not only what they will do on this one-day vacation, but also where, when, and how they will do it. When this occurs, it is usually done sincerely in the name of modesty, enclosure, propriety, or preservation of religious spirit, but it can make a hoax of an otherwise serious and mature situation, and defeat the fundamental purpose of rules and customs in religious life. Generally, measures regulating apostolic work for sisters should allow them to do what lay women of comparable professional and social status would be permitted to do under similar circumstances.

If abuses are evident in the keeping of the rules in religious life, attention should be given to them on an individual basis. Too often new rules are made to counteract violations of rules of which only a few sisters are guilty. Those few individuals should be corrected privately, when necessary, and if the original rule or permission is purposeful, it should remain for the benefit of the other sisters.

Changing the details of conventual rules or customary prescriptions in any instance does not necessarily modify the essence of their meaning. It is necessary, first of all, to examine the purpose of these regulations, and then to design them practically within the limits of a contemporary setting. Consider the matter of great silence, for instance. At the foundation of the Community decades ago, the great silence

might satisfactorily have been scheduled to begin at 7 p.m.
It is reasonable to suppose that the foundress considered
this arrangement in line with prevailing cultural standards.
That was the time the work of the apostolate was com-
pleted for the day. But in the last half of the 20th century,
it is highly improbable that 7 p.m. is a suitable time for
most sisters to begin the great silence. To attempt to do so
would defeat the purpose of the practice. Under these conditions, sisters might be forced by the pressure of apostolic
obligations to violate the great silence regularly. Thus this
conventual prescription would become "a rule for the sake
of a rule" and lead to conscience turmoil instead of the
peace for which it was intended.

The purpose of the great silence is to provide time for
recollection and study, and for referring thoughts to God in
a special way before retiring, as remote preparation for the
morning meditation and Holy Mass. This should be the last
act of the day for a sister after her apostolic duties are com-
pleted and she is ready to retire. This is an important aspect of religious living. A sister's personal love for Christ
prompts her to want to do this. But it is possible that if she
is really to fulfill this purpose, she needs to communicate
with someone and that the evening is the only time available. So if the great silence is to be adapted realistically,
it should begin at the end of the apostolic day for sisters.

Perhaps this should even be arranged on an individual
basis when the active apostolate—the contact with people
in and out of the community—ends for a sister. This may be
at 10:45 p.m. when she returns to the convent from giving
a demonstration in primary reading to a PTA group; or

at 9:30 p.m. when she has finished planning menus for the week and meeting with her staff in the Motherhouse kitchen; or at 9:45 p.m. when she has checked the last set of arithmetic papers; or at 10:30 p.m. when she is free to leave the post-operative patient in the recovery room of the hospital; or at 10 p.m. when she completes her evening class in adult education in a college or a discussion session in a University Newman center. And it is possible that on some rare days, a sister may enjoy the luxury of being ready to retire to her room for quiet study and contemplation at the blessedly early hour of 7 p.m. Sisters must always avoid deifying a means so that it becomes holiness for them rather than only an instrument of it.

Often sisters tend to make only superficial innovations in conventual living which really are not adaptation in the real sense of the term. Most of the time these are sincere efforts to accomplish the recommendations of the Church, but sisters fail to see the discrepancy between substantial principles of Christian charity and the regulations they establish, presumably to accomplish this charity. Sisters sometimes think, for instance, that they have changed their habits when they have reduced a 12 inch hem to 5 inches; that they have adjusted the horarium by changing the hour of rising from 4:50 a.m. to 5:30 a.m.; that they have adapted rules of enclosure when they specify in detail the occasions when sisters may dine out of the convent, or share a coffee hour with lay people at a group meeting. These changes simply indicate circumstances which are different from those prevailing previously, but which are not necessarily, of themselves, substantial modifications that will promote the cause of love in the apostolate.

The sister in the ecumenical age of the Church understands that adaptation means, rather, an insightful understanding of the human needs of sisters and an astute evaluation of the demands of an ever-changing apostolate. Those responsible for executing changes must be capable of sorting the relevant from the irrelevant and the important from the unimportant in apostolic living for sisters. This requires enlarged thinking and perceptive vision.

Community Awareness

The contemporary sister needs to possess an *esprit de corps* which includes the Christian community—all people, religious and lay alike. This spirit of Christian community consciousness is one of total expansiveness and inclusiveness which means strong regard for the honor and concerns of the group. An apostolic commitment of love, not personal convenience and expediency, becomes the norm for community action. This Christian *esprit de corps* is as large as the Heart of Christ, and demands a magnanimity of heart and mind which is great—and not always easy for human persons to acquire. Possessed of apostolic courage, the sister in the modern world habitually asks herself, "What can I give?" rather than "What will I get?" in her approach to life. Christian community awareness enables a sister to be aware of the needs of others as she translates "bear one another's burdens" into practical terms, whether it be in her own conventual family, her Community at large, her field of professional work, the parish, the nation, or the world in general.

Christian community spirit, both in the conventual and the apostolic families, signifies a communion of purposes, ideas, intentions,—a union of love which truly is an extension of the love of Christ in the Eucharist. Love of God and people is the purpose of Christian community action on any level. It implies the freedom of wholesome involvement in which a sister gives her real self to others and is able to accept the genuine from them.

A community always derives its efficacy from the individuals who are its constituents. The specific vitality of a community comes from the combined vigor of the persons who comprise it, and its distinguishing character is determined by the blending of the separate personalities sharing this psychological commonality. This puts the responsibility on the individuals, rather than on a collectivism of any kind. In the Christian community, there is no mass conscience, no group mold, no totalitarian formation, no *en masse* thinking, which could make the group vulnerable to manipulation by the noisy, domineering, or clever members.

For too long the tone of community living in some convents has been set by the sisters with the loudest voices, those who comprise the largest clique, those whose invectives are sharpest, or those whose suavity is most subtle, instead of by those who live rationally as Christian women. Domination of life by the deviant or urbane elements in a religious community can work havoc in common living. Continued tyranny of this type, no matter how cultured it may appear outwardly, can kill the spirit of even the strongest sisters. Most sisters who are mature women want to live the religious vocation as it ought to be lived, and they should insist on deciding the caliber of their life in community. Sister Moody, Sister Cantankerous, Sister Self-pity, or sisters habitually afflicted with any of the other varieties of "birdhouse" maladies should, under no circumstances, be given leeway to determine community atmosphere or practices. Psychologically, these sisters are only cardboard giants or tissue paper puppets. Their oppressive or cunning tactics of whatever nature, invulnerable as they may appear, are fickle and can be punctured with comparative surety by honest confrontation. Sometimes this confrontation should be made by superiors; at other times, sisters who are subordinates can best execute this task and should receive the support of the superior's authority.

Mature religious women have the duty to take the initiative in fixing the terms of congenial, peaceful community living, and should be adamant in enforcing them. They should never be intimidated into inaction by the threats and denunciations of those sisters who know only a nominal apostolic commitment. Sisters who are social hazards in community life must, therefore, be made to understand that, under no conditions, will their unpredictable and unchristian conduct be the blueprint for community life. They must be faced directly and fearlessly by mature sisters— either by the superior herself or by sister subjects with the blessing of the superior; and be assured in clear *ultimatum* that they must either learn to cooperate reasonably or withdraw quietly from the community situation. Thus, with no alternative but to make substantial efforts to live maturely, they will never again feel so comfortable in pursuing their deviant ways. Besides, they will be forced to discover a more effective way of life. This is the beginning, at least, of improved community living.

This type of social pressure is one of the greatest, even though not the easiest, acts of charity a sister can perform for members of her Community. This disciplinary interaction between sisters always is characterized by the propriety and dignity becoming cultured Christians. It is honest, but never brutal; resolute, but not relentless; exacting, but in no way unforgiving. According to the standards of militant Christian love, it is incredible that a mature sister would ever justify immature and/or discourteous actions as suitable retaliative or corrective responses to the uncharitable digressions of her companion sisters in community life. Sisters who use childish, emotionally explosive, or crafty means of controlling a group situation, usually are deluded and do not really want to be that way, but find themselves trapped, as it were, by their ungoverned emotions. Notwithstanding all evidence to the contrary, they actually expect their mature companion sisters to exert on them the self-discipline they would like to possess.

It is true, human beings cannot change patterns of living over night. In amending their ways, these sisters need the patience and kindness, as well as the firmness, of their companions. Community power depends on the degree to which individual uniqueness is developed and made to yield apostolic dividends through intelligent human living and service. The total community will be as strong and prolific as its individual members. It is imperative, then, that no sister feel entitled to indulge selfishness or chicanery of any brand, but rather that she be spurred to intensive efforts to become a powerful and serene minister of Christian love in her Community.

Communal life in the Christian sense takes its life-blood from the theological virtues—faith, through which a sister becomes capable of knowing and believing the love of Christ; hope, through which she has power to be secure in anticipating His help and confident in expecting the rewards of love which He has promised; and charity, through which her full humanness is released for loving Him and all His people.

A sister realizes that there is no conflict between the personal and social elements of perfection for her since, if she is real, her love for Christ keeps pace with and can be gauged by her love for people. A sister appreciates the importance of her role in the Mystical Body, knowing that any personal contribution she makes through Christian love affects the whole mystical organism.

A sister should consider conventual communal life from this Christian viewpoint, and define specifics in this light. For example, family spirit in a religious community is a oneness in love, not the dehumanization of having to be together physically all the time. In some instances, the "togetherness" of community life has been misinterpreted to the detriment of the very spirit it aimed to build. Sisters are human, and because they work constantly with people in a social apostolate, it is essential for them sometimes to get way from people, so that they may be able to live more smoothly with them. Every sister should enjoy the privacy of a room of her own and should avail herself of the opportunity to use it. Just being alone periodically to read,

think, pray, study, or rest is a form of psychological recreation, and is, perhaps, more necessary for a sister's general
well-being than the formally prescribed periods of community recreation. This is not a luxury in the twentieth century. It is an absolute necessity for every sister!

It takes considerable maturity and peace of mind to be
able to live comfortably with oneself, without the tangible
and physical support of a group. It may well be that
some sisters have grown so accustomed to the physical
support of the group in conventual living that they cannot
feel secure, and therefore not peaceful, in the solitude of a
private room. These sisters should be encouraged to develop more personal independence.

A certain social atmosphere is established in community
living by creating an environment of acceptance and "belonging"—the "its-good-to-be-here" feeling developed when
there is genuine love, whole-hearted participation, and con-
tributive giving among sisters in a religious community.
This does not, by any means, indicate common agreement
on all points of view. Community spirit in a conventual
family can never be the same as the affectional relationships
in a natural family group, but it can be comparable. The
same principles of Christian love which govern good natural
family life are those which also direct healthy community
life for sisters; that is, mutual respect and love for each
other regardless of age, competence, occupation, personal
qualities, reciprocal loyalty and congeniality, eagerness to
assist each other without invading personal privacy, sharing
of joys and burdens, open-minded communication of ideas,
and the freedom to be oneself.

A sister should go into a community with the attitude that she will love her sisters and, hopefully, in turn be loved by them. This attitude prevails also as she goes to her class, to the sick in a hospital, or to those she contacts in any other apostolic work. Such an expectation sets the tone for vital apostolic functioning. According to the laws of human averages, a sister can expect much good in all persons, and if she is honest in looking for it, she will find it. If she really allows herself to know people individually and learns to identify each one with his good qualities, she will experience minimal difficulty in appreciating them, even though she may not agree with them. This benevolent attitude will lessen irritations and disruptions in human interaction which may otherwise result from conflicting personal qualities.

Further, if the sister in the contemporary world had genuine concern for the Church, in general, she would, for instance, be more openminded in recruiting vocations to religious life. As of now, she tends to limit her vocational concerns to her own vested interests—her religious community—and often to the detriment of the aspirant in particular and the apostolate in general.

If a student who is interested in nursing wants to be a Religious and seeks advice from a sister in a community devoted exclusively to teaching, the sister, if she is honest and primarily interested in the welfare of the apostolate, will have to inform the student truthfully of the type of nursing done in the community. If she has the real Christian *esprit de corps,* she will suggest to the young woman that she join a community where hospital nursing is done

—or at least indicate the advisability of investigating this possibility. This breadth of vision and selfless love of the apostolate would be advantageous both to the cause of God and to the personal sanctification of the aspirant concerned. And God, in His great and just love, will undoubtedly, adequately reward such generous charity.

The more Christian community awareness is developed, the more sisters will be willing to combine their efforts— in the formation of sisters and in other apostolic endeavors. Inter-community and intra-community rivalries and insecurities will be notably decreased, at least, if not totally abandoned. Sisters who, because of a certain provincialism now hestiate to centralize their resources, will consider the advisability of pooling assets—personal and financial—for the benefits of the apostolate. In the last fifteen years, great progress has been made in this type of communication and sisters of various communities have braved the escapade of "looking over the psychological walls" at each other. They have been remarkably delighted to find such wonderful people in convents. In fact, now since they are no longer afraid to share, they have actually come to love each other. These strong bonds of filial inter-community affection help to unify the crusade of love. Sisters are drawn closer together by the only force that counts. They are no longer fearful of what they may be losing by broadening their limits of cooperation, but are grateful for what they and the whole world are gaining.

Christian Communication

Social Responsibility

In order to establish the foundations for social responsibility in Christian love, it is necessary to recapitulate basic ideas. A sister is a human being—a Christian woman—who has become a Religious apostle. Every aspect of this definition colors what a sister ought to be. As a human being, she is dynamic by nature; she must always be moving either toward becoming a better person, or regressing to a less holy state. As a woman, she is particularly equipped by God for the total dedication of Christian love to which she was formally initiated in Baptism, and later fortified with the militant strength of the graces of Confirmation. As a Religious, she has accepted God's invitation to love Him and people, not only by precept, but also according to the prescriptions of the evangelical counsels in religious life. She either accomplishes her primary purpose—Christian love—by breaking the alabaster potential of her love in a human way, functioning fully in dedicated apostolic involvement, or she succumbs to a numbed existence in which the basic wholeness of her total humanness eventually is made ineffectual or, perhaps, even destroyed.

The obligation of this complete Christian communication presupposes several facts. A sister must be a clear channel of love. She must be apostolically unhampered by neurotic self-centeredness, eager to capitalize on opportunities to transmit Christ to others, and discriminating and free in choosing appropriate media through which she can translate His message in understandable terms. The idea of commitment is fundamentally one of self-action and self-surrender. This means that under the direction of the Holy Spirit, a sister makes herself real in a Christian sense, and gives herself, and not just her possessions, to God and, through Him, to others. It is this unconditional gift of self to God in Christian love which makes dedicated virginity possible. It should make a sister more human, more like God, more capable of loving others as she crystallizes her own identity in His image.

A religious woman is, therefore, expected to give witness to Christ in a human way. This is for her a social responsibility which originates in the essence of her commitment as a religious apostle. A sister must consciously devote herself to the truth of this genuine commitment, lest she be tricked into the pseudo-dedication of self-worship. She violates her commitment if she lives selfishly, striving for personal perfection as a solitary goal, without understanding her obligation of extending herself apostolically. It is true, the sister apostle endeavors seriously and consistently in a human Christian way, to attain the degree of Christlikeness that is possible for her. But she must also constantly be aware of her responsibility for sharing the fruits of her personal perfection with others through Christian service.

People take for granted that what a sister is, should be identical with what Christ is, and if they find glaring and continual discrepancies in this identity, they plead with her to live what she professes. (Incidentally, the layman does not lack credentials to evaluate a sister—he works continually with her and is in a most strategic position to assess her value as a bearer of the love of Christ!) A sister must sell her product—the love of Christ—not in words alone, but in action, dignified by the strength of God. She must sympathize with people, appreciate their joys, share their poverty, encourage their efforts, be patient with their mistakes, discuss ideas with them. This is a day-by-day, lifelong process for a sister—every moment, whether she is alone, in community, or working in the apostolate—she is advertising Christian love and all the things for which it stands. Since people are looking for Christ, and since they are not always finding Him in religious women, they logically conclude that perhaps sisters could communicate His message better if they had less rigid rules of enclosure, visited homes more frequently, changed their conventual garb or their field of apostolic activity, or any of the other suggestions currently being made in the name of adaptation.

People are struggling to help sisters understand their problems as they affect the social apostolate. The truth is, however, lay people are not eager to have sisters as guests in their living rooms or at their dining tables, nor do they want to meet them at public recreation centers or at the civic opera house. Further, they are not interested in sipping cocktails with sisters in a discotheque or in shouting cheers with them in the baseball park. They are looking for Christ, and they expect that sisters have Him because they publicly proclaim this fact through their mode of life.

On the other hand, truly militant and mature sisters are not looking for ultimate perfection in each other or in communal living, nor are they seeking luxurious conveniences in living accommodations and apostolic environment. Neither are they asking for wholesale mitigations in conventual regulations. Nor are they questioning the validity of the Christian spirit of a genuine religious vocation—or of its traditional implementation, for that matter. They are only asking the questions about current practices of Christian love in conventual life which should have been asked long ago. They are pleading that circumstances be arranged so Christian love can be practiced freely, humanly, productively by them. They want to be allowed and encouraged to communicate responsibly and in a Christian manner with their sisters in community and with all people.

What a sister is, is so evident to those with whom she works and with whom she lives, that they don't hear what she says she is or ought to be. If sisters say they are women in love with Christ, others expect them consistently to produce concrete evidence of this in kindness, understanding, justice, honesty, and Christian poise in their daily person-to-person contacts. A sister's humanness—her ability to love, her readiness to laugh, her reasonable concern for rest, relaxation, enjoyment, her diligent work, her warm congeniality and tender compassion, her strength in suffering, her sincerity in communicating with others—all indicate her love of Christ as a person, and her willingness to radiate it to others.

Without these inevitable marks of real love of God and people, erudition and skill of any kind become only pompous display and prevent the sister from being an agent of love who can touch the hearts of others and inspire them to strive for Christian fulfillment. A sister, therefore, needs to attend to the particulars of practical Christian love as they apply specifically to her personal life and to her apostolate.

Authentic Christian Fellowship

Real Christian love must be evident in the group most immediate to a sister's activities. If a sister really loves people and is interested in them, it will be apparent. The love that doesn't "show" is not worth its name. Besides, according to the laws which govern it, Christian love must be articulated by a sister in ways which consistently bear out its meaning and depth. A sister must beware of the possibility of fooling herself by excusing the contradictions in her loving.

Real Christian love is a foreigner to any type of exploitation and condescension. It never caters or patronizes. If ever love is feigned under these guises, the ruse soon is exposed and the protestations of love ring hollow. Legalized selfishness makes love sterile, because love cannot be codified according to rigid and selfish standards. For a time, a sister may be comfortably deluded by living whimsically in fulfilling her duty of loving people. She can say "I'll pray for you" or "you can use anyting I have—just don't ask for my time." Thus, on the basis of possessing "supernatural" love, she attempts to justify her selfish unwillingness to be inconvenienced. Or she may say "I love everybody in the same way" or "I'm nice to everyone—but I don't get involved with them." In this way she tries to legitimatize her indifference to people with cries of impartiality or detachment. In saying "I make everybody feel good by always agreeing with them and complimenting them," she may be defending the insincerity of her flattery and condescension by pretending that it serves a noble purpose. In all this, she can convince herself that she is striving for the genuine influence of Christian love.

The day of self-reckoning is bound to come, however, when she can no longer live peacefully with herself and others. She must make a choice of alternatives. Either she will continue to suffer the tensions and confusions of a mock-Christianity, or she will endeavor to develop an authentic Christian fellowship with people. If she is really to communicate Christian love to others, she must possess the qualities peculiar to militant apostolicity: sincerity and generosity.

Sincerity

A mature sister apostle knows God and trusts His unfailing love for her. By keeping her life focus sharply directed to Him, she gives meaning to the circumstances in her life, particularly to those she can neither understand nor change. No matter how distracted, harassed, or absorbed she becomes in her apostolate, she always sees through, over, above, around, or beyond people and situations to Him. She knows the truth of her relations with God, and does not smugly conclude that emotional elation in prayer is mysticism, or vainly confuse a self-centered complexity of pious externals with the purity of substantial spirituality emanating from the simplicity of real Christian love. Through this

Christian optimism, her fundamental attitudes remain un-
changed so she can be resilient in intelligent forbearance of
pain, and happy in concentrating on the blessings of her
life.

If a sister fails to live Christian love in a vibrant way,
she is never really at peace. She is always experiencing a
gnawing yearning for something she does not have, or cannot have, or should not have, while overlooking the satisfactions of what she does have. She develops a type of inverted
trust by which she questions God's sincerity when He is
good to her. When she receives blessings, she immediately
wonders if there is a "rose blooming" for her or how long
it will be until He sends the cross. This, of course, will most
likely also be the pattern of her reactions to people. If a
person is kind to her and shows love, she may automatically suspect him of ulterior or unworthy motives.

The psychologically stable sister apostle nurtures a holy
reverence for persons and things because she considers them
as they relate to God and not only as they affect her. This
gives her an objectivity which makes a challenging adventure of the discovery of God everywhere and in everyone.
She has courage—enough fear of God to make her prudent,
and sufficient faith in Him and people to make her strong.
She is daring in taking the risks involved in exerting influence on others through Christian love, and patient in
waiting God's good pleasure in arranging the circumstances
of her life. She is concerned only about discovering what
He expects of her in any instance of her life, and prompt
in accomplishing it. If she is to attain tranquillity of spirit,
she must really be honest in identifying and developing the

real in herself. Further, she must realize the magnitude of her apostolic duty to expend herself in loving service for others.

A sister may find that constant devotion to these tasks may not only be difficult, but even humanly repugnant, but she reaps strength and satisfaction from the personal integrity and Christian wholeness which result from lavish self-giving in genuine commitment to God. Refusal to know and to accept herself as she is, is tragic insincerity, and a sister must aim to be what she can become before God, and not only what others think she should be. Ultimately, she is what she is before God and not what men think she is. Truth stands on its own merits and needs neither to be justified nor vindicated. It can afford to be silent.

The sister who is not living sincerely takes the unreal and attempts to make it real, or makes an illusion of the real and allows her actions to be dominated accordingly. Since she does not understand love, she becomes a victim of her delusions which dictate the pattern of her interaction with others. One of the delusions is a surface show of openness or straightforwardness which may even amount to social barbarity masquerading as frankness. It may not be sincerity at all, but only a hurting cruelty resulting from insincerity and/or insecurity. So often insincerity concocts evil when there is none, to satisfy a selfish satisfaction or self-pity. Brutality is never honesty. A sister cannot indulge personal faults and feelings to crush the spirits of other people. Excuses for selfishness prevent her from loving and keep her a prisoner of her whims and fickleness.

When a sister makes a genuine commitment of love to

God she can appreciate relative values and make choices accordingly. She can habitually respond maturely to reasonable motivation, and make correct judgments about herself and others. This regular pattern of rational living makes her tranquil and free from fear, anxiety, and unhappiness. The sister who is deeply chaste—that is, who profoundly loves God and people—is not easily scandalized. She has no need either to be righteous or shocked. She can approximate God's view of real sin and actual wrongdoing, so she does not impute evil where there is none, nor does she exaggerate what actually exists. She is free of compulsive obligations to classify all of life in categories of morality. She is not a slave to personal indignation or phantastic misinterpretations. She is free; and free acts are integrating.

Fear can only prevent the action of love. The sister who does not understand Christian love, allows her sins and "challenges" to mar her union with God because she cannot overcome the shame and guilt feelings without damage to her love. For the same reason, she may allow her natural aversions for the "challenges" of others and/or the misunderstandings of normal human associations to hurt or to destroy her charitable fellowship with people. The sister who loves, on the other hand, realizes that sin can be the beginning of loving God more as was the case with Mary Magdalen, and knows that wholesome, trusting relationships between people can be born of the pain of disagreements and antipathies as in the case of Paul of Tarsus. The sister who is real accepts herself as she is, and loves people as they are. Her own sins and shortcomings make her more dependent on God and spur her to more diligence in becoming a saint, and the transgressions and "challenges" of others only inspire her with greater Christian compassion and understanding.

From time to time, the well-balanced sister needs to retire psychologically to a realm of quiet. She needs solitude. She can find this in a metropolitan subway on her way home from an evening class, as well as in the undisturbed quiet of the great silence. She takes time to sit back within herself, as it were, detached for the time being from the hubbub of life, to make unbiased appraisals of herself and her commitments. She has sufficient self-knowledge so she can be comfortable and peaceful when she is alone. She develops the art of recollection, the ability to retreat purposefully from activity, so she has time to look around perceptively and decide who she is and what she wants to become. It gives her the vision to avoid such absorption into a group or the environment that she loses herself in this identification, accepting group standards without question. She must develop enough healthy personal independence so she can be creatively autonomous and productively free from the group mold. She must be herself. Besides, all this has to be in line with the prescriptions of religious vows and rules.

It is necessary that she keep silence so it is quiet enough to think—to create! Silence, for a sister, does not necessarily always mean an absence of words, but a balanced alignment of all her life with God so that she is free of habitually noisy and disturbing clashes of motive, actions, or emotional responses. For decades, silence has been wisely prescribed as part of the religious life. In silence, a great sister apostle daily comes to a deeper understanding of God, herself, and others through meditative prayer. She utilizes the opportunity of silence not only to dream dreams of apostolic significance, but also to plan ways of fulfilling them. Too often, however, undue emphasis has been put on externals without emphasizing the purposeful activities of silence. Since sisters have often interpreted silence to mean only a lack of oral communication, there is much keeping of silence for silence' sake in convents.

It is possible for a sister to observe the externals of silence without ever experiencing real quiet. Without self-government, meticulous keeping of conventual silence can be an escape from reality for a sister. It can bring the torture of self-hatred or provide proper climate and sufficient time for emotional jamborees of various sorts: rash judgments, withering self-pity, petty resentments, seething hostilities, or sullen moodiness.

Generosity

The mature sister communicates Christian love through a service permeated with generosity and self-sacrifice. She is generous in cooperative duty. She always asks herself how she can serve rather than how she can be served. If she is really interested in the cause, and not just a slave to her own convenience and whims or to her own ideas, she will contribute her services without undue concern as to who will receive the credit. She will allow the person with the best qualifications to do the task at hand, and she will offer herself wherever her talents can be utilized most effectively She will volunteer her assistance and not wait to be invited to contribute or to be coaxed into action. She will be as ready to give of what she is—her understanding, consideration, patience, trust, appreciation, forgiveness—as of the objects she possesses. This real giving of self is true Christian generosity, and always involves risks: of being unaccepted and unappreciated, of possible failure, or of being selfishly taken advantage of by others.

Generosity also means real humility in taking advice. There always is the possibility that "I don't know everything." Also, it is important that a sister apostle be flexible so she can progress and improve her approach in her apostolate, since "things may have changed for the better since I learned how."

Courtesy, a graciousness of human interaction, is based on respect for the dignity of others as human beings. This is more than a mechanical saying of "please," "thank you," or "excuse me." These can become wooden niceties which are meaningless, cultured formalities if they are not prompted by gracious warmth which typifies real love. A sister should learn to love people and to educate herself to look for the good in all of them. Christian love purifies her vision so she can take Christ's view of people. Vicariously, she participates in and expresses His individualized love for each person. She should show all people the courtesy they deserve because they are human persons.

The mature sister has functional humility so she sees the truth of things. Since she can accept herself, she can also accept others, even when she is not naturally attracted to them. She respects all people, regardless of accidental factors as personal attractiveness, color, creed, age, beauty, position, or competence. Courtesy should be constant and spontaneous. It implies a certain gentleness and warmth—a dignified approach to others. Too often a sister erects psychological pedestals on status lines, as it were, on which she puts people in rank order of presumed personal worth.

According to this artificial hierarchy of assigned personal value, the superior takes precedence over the principal of the high school, so she is treated with greater respect and courtesy. The Bishop is rated more highly than the young curate who assists the pastor, so he is welcomed to the convent with much more social fanfare. Or the sisters with whom she lives are less important status-wise than sister guests from other Communities or than the Mother Provincial of her own Community, so they are the recipients of only a left-over courtesy, if they get much at all; while professional visitors from state departments receive more deference than the parents of students.

People with whom a sister lives and works have a first right to her love and courtesy. Evidences of love which are "saved" for visitors, for next year's class, for the Reverend Mother's annual visitation, or for the superior's nameday are highly questionable. At best, they are only "special occasion" or "important personage" proprieties which can be taken out for display at will. Such mechanically regulated sentiment may be diplomacy or politics, but it surely is not Christian love.

If a sister thinks kindly of others habitually, it will not be difficult for her to be kind to them. The giving of real kindness does not depend on liking people or in agreeing with them. It implies a mature acceptance of them as they are, and an open-minded understanding of them as individuals.

Courtesy is such things as the interested attention to another's relation of news, the finesse of best table manners used daily at the convent table (and not only at the banquets of the year when sisters enjoy luncheon at a hotel during the annual teachers' convention!), the sincerity of a gracious refusal, the propriety in choosing language in a disagreement, the tone of voice in making a request, the gentility of social etiquette in requesting and acknowledging hospitality, and the smile and warmth of greeting others.

Praise can be a most uplifting expression of love. A sister should not be afraid to recognize the talents of others. So often the ridiculous notion prevails that if people are complimented, they will become proud or vain. All persons need honest recognition of their accomplishments, particularly by those of their own family and friends. Therefore, a sister needs to be appreciated and loved for herself by her superiors and sister companions. This familial support of love and loyalty is essential to her psychological well-being, and nothing can be substituted for it.

Roses of praise offered to a sister only when she is resting in a mortuary chapel become ironic testimony of an aborted Christian love and are much too late either to be necessary or comforting. Praise and recognition will be genuine if they are honest and the mature sister knows how to sift real praise from flattery. Sometimes a sister may not be willing to appreciate others openly for fear that she will lose something for herself. Unfortunately, envy and jealousy often motivate the actions of a sister in this regard.

It seems a tragedy that often the personal or apostolic accomplishments and successes for which a sister is lauded by the public are those for which she suffers the most disdain, rejection, or jealousy from the members of her own household. This can be so painful that it may make a sister afraid or unwilling to continue using her talents advantageously in the apostolate. Most sisters will not accomplish spectacular feats, but there are dozens of opportunities regularly to acknowledge their everyday achievements.

A sister who communicates Christian love is warm, friendly, and gracious in her dealings with others. She is reasonably even-tempered. A sister who loves is approachable to those with whom she works. One does not have to speculate about her current mood before asking her a question or speaking with her. She is predictable because things in her life are in good order. She is optimistic and cheerful. This does not imply that she is hilarious or giddy. Surely the mature woman is not the slap-stick quipper to whom one can never speak without receiving a smart retort, nor is she the person who has no troubles. She knows that at times life can become complicated with human problems and annoyances. She cultivates a genuine sense of humor, however, seeing and appreciating the difference between what is and what ought to be, and enjoying the discrepancy. She can laugh—at least quietly and privately, if need be. If she cannot manage to laugh, she will at least be able to smile. A hearty laugh or a smile often helps to take the edge from an unpleasant situation. Frequently, a sense of humor enables a sister not only to know what to see and hear in human relations, but when, and directs her in deciding whether she should give a message with words or only with a look. This Christian perspective helps a sister keep things in right order of precedence. She learns to distinguish between what is really important and what may be important only to her. Sometimes life's events deserve no more than a laugh—even at herself.

The smile is a wonderful agent of love in human association, and has power to lubricate friction in human relations. A sister should always smile, or at least be ready to smile. There is so much in life to be happy about that a sister ought to be continually joyous. People always are more important than things, and deserve the very best preferential treatment. In fact things assume importance only to the degree that they can serve people. A sister should learn to respect the dignity of each human being with whom she works, and to be considerately aware of him as an individual with unique qualities and needs. This interest must be given honestly in the spirit of true Christian love. There is nothing more despicable in human relationships than to misuse someone's affection or to be dishonest in giving love to another.

If a sister is approached by a person, let her give undivided attention to him—really listen to what he has to say. It is possible to give someone time without really hearing what he says, or to look at him without actually seeing him. It is most disconcerting, for instance, for a sister to ask for something when the superior continues to look at the newspaper, already is reaching for the next job she has to do, or sighs audibly with a half-smile and a manner that says "I'm-busy—don't-bother-me-now." The child who is always made to feel that the teacher is too busy to talk to him will soon stop approaching her. Likewise, the sister who always finds her superior too busy to give permissions will be tempted to do things without bothering to get the permission.

Accessibility is another side of approachability. Sister apostles must be available when people need them. Teaching sisters are not making themselves realistically available when they are willing to receive phone calls from parents only from 6-7 p.m. on school days. In the first place, the family dinner hour may be from 6-7 p.m., and secondly, what should Mrs. Brown do on the days when she discovers only at 8 p.m. that nine-year old Tom doesn't know his homework assignment?

Rejecting a person in cold disdain, even temporarily, is one of the most cruel and depersonalizing actions that can be done to a human being. The psychological dynamics of ignoring a person are these: when you ignore me, you treat me as if I did not exist and that literally kills me psychologically, because you act as if I am nothing. This is quite a contrast to being reprimanded for something. When you scold me, you are treating me as if I am someone. And even if you do not like me, you still think I am at least deserving of your time. And I can take this. The degree of love one has for the person who is cold determines the damage done by his rejection. If coldness from a loved one persists over a prolonged period of time, it is possible that a person will suffer irreparable harm to his self-concept. It is always much more satisfactory—and more human—to discuss matters, even vehemently, if necessary, than to indicate by coldness that something is awry, without giving some explanation or some opportunity for the person concerned to vindicate his position or to admit his error.

A mature sister is genuinely kind and considerate of others. She develops a sensitivity to the feelings of others and treats them as she wishes to be treated. Understanding is genuine sympathy for others—the "I-know-how-you-feel" attitude. This combination of empathy and compassion is the quality with which a sister apostle is able and willing to view the problems of others from their vantage point. To love another enough to know really how he feels about something is true giving of self. It is entering into that person, as it were, to see, hear, and feel things as he does. It does not necessarily mean that one agrees with him.

Understanding is the key to working successfully with people, and can be deepened by experience and suffering. This aspect of Christian love helps a sister to know the joys and problems of others. Too often a sister thinks only of sharing the sorrows of others. Sometimes it is necessary that someone share their joys. Attempting to understand how others feel prevents rash judgments. Things are not always as they seem to be on the surface. Never judge—just understand—is a good guidepost for working well with people. If a sister would understand, she would learn to be more prudent in minding-her-own-business and in evaluating people and circumstances only after she has heard all sides of any issue. So often the peripheral judgments made without sufficient or correct facts, but only on the indiscrete or distorted appraisals of others, are hazardous in working with people. People must be accepted as they are, and if a sister expects to help others, she must try to understand them. On occasion, it may be necessary for a sister to assist someone to reconsider a situation in new perspective and with new insights, so he can make new decisions and take more orderly action. But the sister remains aware of the person as an individual, and is respectful of his feelings and reactions. Each person is important because he is John or Mary or Susie. Each one wants to be accepted by others because he is himself. It is devastating to people to be consistently known as "the eighth grade teacher," "the principal," "Tom's little brother," or "the sister who cooks." Each one wants to be known by name and to be appreciated as an individual person.

Another important aspect of understanding people and accepting them as they are is allowing them to achieve at their own rate and according to their particular potential. Each one should be challenged to work to his capacity. It is psychologically disastrous constantly to compare a student, for instance, to someone else—whether it is a member of his family, another student in the class, or even to his performance in another situation. Likewise, it can be discouraging for a sister when her performance in any task is perpetually contrasted to that of her predecessor.

The more a sister can understand, the less need there will be to criticize uncharitably. Understanding nurtures patience with others. A mature sister is willing to give people time to make mistakes so they can learn, and to trust that they can profit by these errors and improve. An understanding sister knows that any human problem is possible to human beings, and what may look malicious externally may really not be so motivationally. If it were possible to measure malice tangibly, it would be surprising to observe the little vicious ill will of which people really are guilty, even though at times their conduct portrays a sickening evidence of exterior malevolence of various types.

Honesty is a special feature of Christian love and really stems from a sister's being real. She knows who she is, what she thinks, why she thinks it, and lives according to her convictions. This sets the tone for community living. Everybody is "safe" with everyone else. There is a wholesome freedom of expression which allows for intelligent disagreement and diversity of thinking. When all persons in a group consistently think alike about all topics, no one really thinks very much or very profoundly about any of them.

A sister must trust others. It is better to give the benefit of the doubt and then to realize that trust was not deserved, than to mistrust when trust is in order. A sister must take for granted that others are sincere until they prove they are not. Mistrusting a person without reasonable cause constitutes a grave insult to him because it carries incriminating insinuations against his integrity. An impregnable obstacle to Christian interpersonal relations may be developed through continued and unrelenting suspicion and doubt which intensifies the enmity of the person who is skeptical and generates an injurious loss of self-confidence and sense of self-identity in the one who is mistrusted.

Respect for the privacy of others is a matter of honest Christian love. This is especially true in religious life of such things as mail and telephone conversations. Surely every sister is entitled to privacy in these matters, and a certain delicacy of consideration should be afforded to her. Further, a sister should ordinarily be allowed to confide in whomever she wishes. To violate or to force another's confidence is most dishonest. To expose oneself in confidence to another is a sacred thing, and usually can be done only when there is genuine meeting of minds and mutual trust. Unreasonable limits and regulations deny the meaning of giving confidences.

There should be freedom for a sister to speak to those in whom she can confide. This is essential for her as a human being. Postulants, novices, and junior sisters should also be permitted this freedom of conscience. It is unthinkable that young women in their formation programs should be expected to bare their souls to a superior just because she is the directress of a particular department even if she does not inspire their confidence. Ordinarily, if the directress is a mature woman, most young people will not find it difficult to confide in her. But superiors at any level should not feel threatened when a sister wants to confide in someone else, because this does not necessarily indicate rejection. In fact, they should be prudently generous in making arrangements so this freedom of communication is possible for a sister.

Consideration must also be given to the fact that occasionally a sister, a novice, or a postulant may be able to get more help from a member of her peer group than from a superior. When this is the case, the honest superior who is genuinely concerned for the welfare of her subjects and not selfishly devoted to personal prestige, will respect this situation and provide suitable opportunities for communication. A superior, likewise, should be permitted the privilege of confiding in and taking counsel with whomever she wishes.

Communication

A fundamental lack of sincerity and understanding among sisters often makes for a strange, debilitating secrecy in conventual living. This creates a suspicious atmosphere in which problems develop in community life. Too many conventual matters are surreptitiously handled by superiors or, perhaps by their delegates, and often the confidences which ought to be respected are violated and the loyalites which ought to be given are withheld.

Sisters are the religious community and should be knowledgeable about community activities so they can function actively as community members. It is impractical, for instance, for all sisters to attend community chapter meetings, so they elect representatives to discuss and settle community business. Chapter business is really the business of the sisters therefore, and some proceedings should be published for them. To take another example: sisters live closely with each other in community and are in a position to discover leadership qualities in their companions. Major superiors are not able as readily to get this information firsthand. If they would allow sisters to share this knowledge, more capable sisters could be appointed to leadership positions, and the entire face of life in many communities would be substantially changed for the better.

Sisters should be informed about all major community

problems and projects. Sisters who are well-informed about their community will be more vitally interested in it, and more willing to contribute to community welfare. Sisters should always be treated as adults. It is true, there are immature religious women who manage to imprudently publicize community family business to those who have no right to know. These sisters are social liabilities and security risks in a community. They need to overcome the childish impulse to tell everything they know, and to learn the ethics of adult loyalty to family secrets! But most religious women would respond maturely to the trust placed in them by superiors, and through this cooperative approach, it can reasonably be hoped that even sisters who are not mature now will become better.

Superiors need to profit by the competent suggestions of the sisters. In community life, superiors should keep the sisters informed about all matters that are not confidential. Sisters have a right to know community transactions—this makes for a healthy family spirit. On the other hand, affairs that are personal should be respected confidentially. Inquisitiveness can be a "sin" of community living. Even if sisters share a common life, they should enjoy a certain privacy in their lives. Minding another's business in community life is never a virtue even though sometimes it masquerades as such. Sisters who lack a sensitivity to the feelings of others sometimes justify their impropriety by calling it friendly interest or concern. There is a fine line of distinction here and the sister who really loves others considerately is keen in perceiving the demarcation.

Sisters should endeavor to open channels of communication in their communities. They should talk things over. Superiors should collect all the best thinking of the sisters before making major decisions in community life. This would blast the secrecy which, like a psychological smog, so often surrounds even important moves in religious life. If sisters could communicate with each other, freely offer suggestions, compare proposals, share ideas, the community apostolate would profit by the best thinking of all sisters. Sisters do not have to agree, but at least they can be honest and unselfish in disagreeing if they have exposed themselves to all facets of group thinking. This wholesome open-mindedness which means acceptance and respect for the ideas of others would make for more competent functioning on all levels of apostolic living. Besides, it would do much to eliminate prejudice in community living.

Prejudice in conventual circles usually is subtle, but can be more devastating because frequently it assumes the semblance of culture and even can be rationalized in pietistic terms. Conventual prejudices, often inspired by personal jealousies among sisters, are not evidenced in open riots, tear gas sprees, or freedom marches. These would be frightening manifestations of evil for conventual climate and would shock the sensibilities of even the most uncharitable religious women. But Christian love in community life in convents often is dynamited at its foundation by damaging insinuations, half-truths used brutally out of context, rationalizations which acceptably cover the truth for political purposes, calumniating accusations, uncontrolled anger, silent fury of disdain, or some incredible assassination of a person's reputation.

This venting of personal antagonisms and irresponsible actions can be shrouded so carefully in righteousness that, in some instances, their psychologically ruinous nature assumes an aura of goodness, such as zeal for the apostolate, concern for the religious spirit of the community, interest in the personal sanctification of an individual sister, or devotion to the "will of God." Such hostilities can crush the enthusiasm and integrity of a sister who is the victim, alienate sisters from each other, and kill the spirit of Christian love in a religious community.

There is no doubt that such prejudices and biases seeded in community life, seep into the works of the apostolate to poison the influences of sister apostles. This is tragic refusal by sisters to love, and no amount of doing for others replaces the loving to which sisters have committed themselves. If sisters and their apostolic contacts are to be protected from these basic types of uncharitableness, which, in effect, really are forms of cultured diabolism, these conditions must be exposed and counteracted openly and fearlessly in an atmosphere of active Christian love.

Generally speaking, sisters are afraid of each other in many ways. They usually manage to produce a surface display of comfortable social interaction, but for the most part, many of them hesitate really to be themselves in community life. Most of these sisters are not even aware of this reaction in themselves. Whether there is foundation for it or not, many sisters fear reprisal, rejection, opposition, or criticism from their companions, so they tend to be reticent in communicating with others and to shun the consequences of taking an open stand on any issue. Frequently, they are reluctant to take the risks of forming and expressing opinions because they dread the pain of possible failure or rejection. As a result, sisters often play it "safe" and have only casual contact with each other. Other sisters apathetically refuse the responsibility of making appreciative evaluations or critical appraisals of circumstances either because they are discouraged by the failure of previous attempts, or because they think religious obedience dispenses them from this mature Christian obligation. Some sisters never really get to know each other, even though they may live together for a long time, and this may be one reason for the conspicuous lack of stimulating, genuine communication among sisters. Sisters need to take positive measures in dispelling these crippling fears and in razing these blocking barriers between them. They need to be more generous in giving of themselves and in sharing the natural, as well as the spiritual gifts of God.

Color and music are great natural blessings of God to man which certainly can be used advantageously in Christian love in religious life. The drab browns and dull blacks offset by various shades of white and grey which formerly were used so universally in conventual decor were depressing, rather than sanctifying. They have been mercifully replaced in convents by cool blues, hopeful greens, cheery yellows, and soothing pinks!

The powers of reflecting God in a good symphony, or the martial music of a band, or operatic arias cannot be discounted. And who is to undervalue the uplifting potency in the beauty of a floral centerpiece on the refectory table, the colored turkish towel in the bedroom, the harmony of chromatic drapes on the community room windows, or the hominess of a fireplace in the recreation room?

It is important to conventual morale that the finesse of good human living—which is also holy living—be well-used in such mundane aspects of community living as the community meals. For example, sisters should raise the level of eating to that of dining, taking time to enjoy their meals and to socialize with their companions in a relaxed setting. So often sisters rush without apparent purpose through their meals as if they were dispatching an unpleasant task that had to be, accomplished quickly and without much ado. They are so distracted and fatigued that they cannot profit by the reading simultaneously provided to nourish them spiritually.

Sisters should have wholesome and palatable food and be allowed to converse at least at the main meal each day. This would be a wonderful means of recreation and communication which would, in many ways, ease the tensions of common living for sisters. Sisters would find the spiritual reading of their own choice, done privately and when they were more rested, of much more practical value.

Recreation in community life is an exercise prescribed daily for sisters by rule. It is, however, probably one of the most stilted activities of the whole day in many convents. Many sisters accept the recreation period with resignation and blandly "get it over with," but find little renewal of physical and spiritual energy, and practically no stimulation professionally or socially. How can recreation for sisters which now is often only a theoretical reality, really be converted to serve its essential purpose: the periodic regeneration of spiritual, physical, and psychological strength for each sister?

Sisters must give much thought to this conventual problem. Solutions cannot be determined with mathematical precision by a code of laws, or be outlined with autocratic finality by superiors or a delegated group of sisters. Neither can they be confined to the staid limits of existing community traditions. Rather, sisters must be considered as individuals with unique and multi-dimensioned personalities. They have varied personal preferences, tastes, and interests relative to recreation. There are those who sometimes enjoy the wholesome repartee and good fellowship of light conversation and the complete physical relaxation of "just doing nothing" during recreation. On the other hand, there are those who are refreshed by spirited discussion of current items, such as liturgical renewal, war on poverty, racial justice, or conciliar literature. Some sisters can relax daily in the competition of card games, and others will find this a pleasant recreation only on occasion and with certain people. Many sisters will enjoy the excellent programs provided on TV and radio, or be rested by taking time to read current newspapers and magazines. Superiors should take the leadership in discovering and accommodating the recreational preferences of sisters.

The scheduling of the conventual recreation time also needs reconsideration. Is it in the best interests of sisters that formal recreation always follows the evening meal, or for that matter, that it necessarily be at the same time each day? Would the religious spirit of sisters really suffer if the scheduling of daily recreation were arranged on a local

level by the superior and the sisters at a time most profitable for all of them? Is not this type of latitude necessary
if recreation is to be more than a conventional formality
for sisters? In any event, the provision of adequate recreation
for sisters is a community enterprise, and should be regulated by the corporate deliberations and decisions of all
sisters in a community. Contemporary needs of sisters
and their apostolate should govern community recreation.

Conventual Poverty

Religious poverty is a significant aspect of the Christian
communication of love. The vow of poverty taken by a sister should give her perspective in using material things as
means, rather than as ends, in loving God and people.
The renunciation involved in conventual poverty does not
deprive a sister of what she needs to live adequately as a
human being, or of what is reasonably necessary for her
to accomplish apostolic work with facility.

Rather, it should inspire her with a detachment from
selfishness which allows her to appreciate the value of material things, and with the permission of her superiors to
utilize them intelligently in complete living of Christian
love. The sister who really lives Christian detachment in
doing the work of the Church, thoroughly enjoys the good
things of life as blessings from God and profitably uses them
with permission according to the standards of a contemporary apostolate. She sees them as assets in the pursuit of
holiness.

There is, however, a more profound meaning to religious

poverty for a sister. It implies a trusting reliance on God by which she perceives His direction of her in very personal and practical ways. God is a tangible reality to her, and in all occurrences she is conscious of determining what He expects of her. She has the faith to see that His designs for her obviously are in every aspect of her daily life. Therefore, she responds generously, making them pay dividends in the practice of Christian love. She finds Him in the phone calls that come regularly to interrupt her plans, the letters that must be written, the daily recreation in the community room, the guest in the parlor, a visit with a friend, the sudden illness which prostrates her for months, the annual housecleaning, the transfer from a situation where she is loved to one where she is not appreciated, the misunderstanding of a professional associate, the successful math class, the gratitude of the poor, the fatigue and loneliness as well as the joy and peace of apostleship, the smile of a child, the sin of wilfully indulged dishonesty and its consequences, the recalcitrance of a student, or the joy at the conversion of a loved one. She understands that she cannot only love God magnificently through these experiences, but also love His people directly or indirectly as well.

In all her living, the genuine sister apostle, who lives her poverty, is blessed with the singleness of purpose and the intensity of action peculiar to Christian love. She knows that if she is really as poor in spirit as she professes to be, she must love people and care about what happens to them. She must bother about apostolic affairs by exerting responsible influence on her environment, and by making significant apostolic contributions according to her abilities. In all, she must take the initiative to be a truly mature, committed apostle. This is Christian detachment, the foundation of poverty, in which selfishness cannot survive! It helps a sister to make herself real.

She becomes so genuine that she is never so status conscious that she is unwilling to identify with the poor, so degreed that she is condescending to the formally uneducated, so secure in her comforts that she is unsensitive to the anxieties of the destitute, so complacent in her peace and plenty that she cannot grieve with the heartbroken or sacrifice with the deprived, or so righteous that she is disgusted with the rich, the incorrigible, and the unbelieving!

Furthermore, the mature sister who appreciates the essence of her poverty is not so unbearably ego-centered that she cannot abandon private opinion to give service for the common apostolic good, so rigid in her devotion to what has been that she cannot be flexible in adapting to what now must be different, or so myopic in her vision that she cannot tell the difference between the important and the trivial, the sound and the sham in life values!

There are several false ideas which sometimes warp the attitudes of sisters and deter them from a Christian approach to conventual poverty. As a result, sisters can defeat the essential purpose of poverty and violate the basic spirit of Christian love. Ultimately, the work of the apostolate is impeded.

If a sister does not understand how to avoid using things for their own sake, it is possible that she may unwittingly give such undue emphasis to trivia in life, and become so dependent for her satisfactions on material objects or conditions that she becomes actually unhappy when she is deprived of them. For instance, a sister can be so attached to a particular place in the chapel or the refectory that she cannot comfortably make the adjustment when she is assigned to another, or she may so completely "own" the audio-visual equipment provided for her department in the school that she insists on exclusive determination of its use, and resents having to share it with other teachers. Likewise, she may "need" every article advertised for her particular work and not only be unreasonable in demanding them, but become sullen when a superior refuses to indulge her whims.

A sister may come to regard money as a god in the practice of poverty. When this is the case, criteria for conventual poverty are embodied in such expressions as "It didn't cost anything"; "I got it for nothing"; or "I haven't spent a cent"! This sister may become so compulsively dedicated to the saving of money as the essence of her poverty that she is unscrupulous in imposing on the time and money of her lay relatives and friends. The sister who, for example, asks lay people to take her for a long trip by car without compensating them for the expenses involved or without being concerned about the time they must spend away from their work or their families, does not realize that while she has "saved" money for the community, and time for herself, she has been flagrantly unfair to others.

Likewise, the sister who expects gifts from her students which, in most instances, they could not afford to buy for themselves, or who thinks that because she is a sister, she has a right to the free professional services of dentists and doctors, has not reflected on the injustice of her attitudes in these situations. The sister who refuses to give tips according to prevailing customs, always asks about ecclesiastical discounts when making purchases, demands monetary pay for her services to others while expecting favors from them for nothing, expects her status as a religious to warrant her free passage on city transit lines, or who overcharges lay people for the articles they buy in the convent gift shop, has not considered that poverty is also a matter of honesty. Every mature sister should be informed about community finances and must be concerned about the honest increase and prudent expenditure of community funds. She realizes, however, that this is not the epitome of vowed poverty considered in the light of Christian love.

A sister may also suffer a distorted sense of values and falsely identify deprivations, stinginess, or slovenliness with poverty. She may feel that such deprivations as not using proper materials for professional work, having insufficient clothing and food or inadequate living accommodations, in themselves, are true expressions of religious poverty. Further, she may canonize the stinginess of her lack of generosity in sharing her talents, time, or possessions with others without compensation, her unwillingness to contribute to the common good unless she gets something out of it for herself, her refusal to eat on an all-day train trip because she would have to pay for the meals, her fear of making a long-distance phone call to expedite an apostolic procedure, and her evaluation of people and things in terms of the dollar bill. Besides, a sister may feel that her vow of poverty obligates her to be careless about personal appearance.

The mature sister knows that her poverty is not an absence of things, but an effective use of them to further vital Christian living. It is possible that a sister can glory in her deprivations so they become her downfall rather than her sanctification. Stinginess is never a virtue. A sister should have a balanced sense of economy. There may be times in her life when she will understand that she must forego some pleasure or do without something because the community cannot afford it. She must regard her religious community as her family, and make responsible efforts to contribute to its welfare. She has a stable sense of values and knows that money is to be spent wisely for God's purposes, and so she is not afraid to do so with proper authorizations. Such items as a spotless habit, polished shoes, clean linens, correct posture, and personal cleanliness are essential to the spiritual and psychological well-being of every religious woman. Wearing overly patched clothing or keeping clothes beyond their point of utility is not part of poverty. In fact, the waste of time involved in the useless mending and maintenance of these articles is directly opposed to the spirit of religious poverty. True poverty is an essential stepping-stone to the perfection of Christian love.

Religious Obedience

Another important area of communicating Christian love in religious life is in the superior-subordinate relationship established through religious obedience. Obedience is an intelligent and responsible interaction between rational human beings. It takes great personal maturity for a sister to live fruitfully in religious obedience. Obedience in community life is a cooperative effort. It is neither the dependence or submission of a child on the part of a sister, nor is it domination or tyranny on the part of a superior.

Genuine obedience always is mature activity. A sister obeys the directions of a superior or a conventual rule because she loves God. She understands that God often expresses His direction of her through a superior. Superiors are human, so they are not always right or most prudent in their directions, but a sister can use these circumstances to maximum advantage in her life. She gives the superior credit for acting in good faith. She accepts and loves her as a human being, and respects her authority as a superior. She gives her complete filial loyalty. She does not need to agree with the superior, but she must see in her directions the manifest design of God in any particular instance. From the standpoint of expediency, practicality, or prudence, any specific point of obedience may not, in itself, be the most enlightened choice, but it is always the best course of action for the sister concerned. So many aspects of obedience ultimately and intrinsically are matters of personal opinion and really not problems of principle or morality at all, that a mature sister ordinarily can easily maintain emotional and spiritual equilibrium if she maintains the perspective of her commitment to God.

A sister always should be permitted open discussion of a problem with a superior. She may have need of a special type of work because of health, or there may be some family circumstance demanding that she be assigned to work close to her home, or perhaps, far away from it; or she may feel the need for some particular or additional preparation for her apostolic work. In these cases, she has the obligation to discuss it honestly with her superior. It is not fair to expect superiors to be knowledgeable about all things. A sister exerts responsible influence in matters of obedience when necessary and then seriously endeavors to become holy under the circumstances provided.

A sister obeys because she wants to—because she loves Christ and sees obedience as direct communication with Him. She is not forced to obey, in the sense of being "bossed around," nor is she threatened by the possible displeasure of a superior or of the probable discipline she may receive if she refuses to obey. She must be free enough to disobey if she wants to be free enough to choose to obey. Compulsions of any kind deny the essential freedom of religious obedience. Because she loves Christ, a sister can see obedience as a direct operation between herself and Him, with the superior or the rule as mediators. A mature sister is cheerful about obedience. It is not logical to take a vow to love Christ by accepting His will in her regard through superiors and then to complain in sadness and self-pity for the rest of her life, bemoaning the fact that "people are always telling me what to do!"

Blind obedience is not unintelligent submission. It simply means that often the plan of God is not obvious to a sister in the directions she receives from superiors. A superior need not describe all—or any—of the circumstances of her directions to a sister. The sister accepts them without challenging or doubting the motives of the superior. And the superior maturely and sincerely endeavors to function in the best interests of each sister, making sure that her reasons for issuing directives, as well as the directives themselves, are unquestioningly juxtaposed with the principles of Christian love.

Sisters can look to Mary, the Mother of God, for inspiration in obedience as in all other matters of Christian love. Mary enjoyed unmatched purity which made her intense and impeccable in her love for God and people. In all her actions, she evidenced a clarity of purpose, exerted the mature initiative called for by any particular event, and accepted the details of her life with reasoned equanimity rather than with mere passive compliance.

Consider the circumstances of her assignment to the motherhood of God. She listened attentively and open-mindedly, perhaps even a bit apprehensively, to the words of the angel as he relayed God's message to her. Mary was accustomed to rational human reactions. She did her own thinking and was informed about life, so she was puzzled by what she had heard. She knew that if she were to execute God's order correctly she must know what was expected of her. So she respectfully questioned the angel as to how this was to be accomplished since she was not married. After God's design relative to her conception of the Son of God was clarified, she accepted this obedience confidently. She recognized the Providence of God in all circumstances of her life and responded to His love with the strong maturity of a woman, not with the unthinking submission of a child. She was free to choose to obey. Once she had accepted this obedience, she completely committed herself to its fulfillment. Because she understood her subordinate role, she could quietly trust God and function effectively even when He did not explain His total plans for her.

Mary also knew her obligation as a mature woman to exert responsible influence on situations in her life. She felt secure in making suggestions. As she and her Son celebrated with relatives and friends at the wedding at Cana, she was prompted by her womanly sensitivity for the feelings of others to ask her Son to replenish the supply of wine to prevent embarrassment for the hosts. She not only took the initiative to make the recommendation in this instance, but with true feminine confidence in those she loved, she told the steward to do as her Son would direct. Then she waited patiently and trustingly for Him to fulfill her request in His own way. Such is the simplicity of genuine Christian love!

Superiorship

The appointment or election of sisters to leadership positions in religious life is a heavy and serious responsibility for major superiors and electoral groups. The influence of superiors on sisters is penetrating and all-encompassing. Superiorship is an opportunity for the superior herself to love God and people more and for her to help sisters to become holier also. Superiorship is a particularly mature business and may never be looked upon as a burden or as a status symbol. It is disastrous to the community life of sisters as well as for her personally to appoint an immature person as a superior. If a sister is not mature before her assignment to community leadership, ordinarily, she will not become mature as a superior. If a sister superior is insecure, she will be afraid, and will tend to use authority as a weapon, rather than as a means of promoting Christian love. The appointment or election of superiors in religious life should be done because of personal merit, rather than on some arbitrary basis. In every case, the person asked to assume the responsibilities of superiorship should be the most balanced sister who also is adequately qualified by academic and practical experience. It is psychologically catastrophic to everyone concerned to assign the duties of superiorship to a sister merely because she is the eldest, or has the most degrees, or is irreproachably faithful to externals, or has the most influential family background, or is most conservative in her views, or advocates a progressive approach to life.

A religious superior must be a whole and holy woman possessed of a greatness which is habitually evident in her prudence, generosity, sincerity, and courage. She should be a real woman who loves God and people in committed and sanctifying human completeness. Her closeness to Christ should enable her to love people as individually, respectfully, warmly, and honestly as He loves them. She should also be blessed with genuine panoramic vision to see beyond the present, so that the plans she makes and implements today meaningfully affect the tomorrows ahead. She must be unafraid to expeditiously open untried avenues of more timely witnessing of Christ by initiating apostolic projects which mean either an expansion of current tasks for sisters or an introduction to new kinds of work. A religious superior must be capable of intellectual leadership; that is, she must be insightful and objective in assessing people and circumstances, strong and honest in making decisions, and fearless and prudent in following them through.

Genuine humility should make her acutely perceptive in recognizing and utilizing the talents of the sisters under her direction for the best interests of the people of God's kingdom. Christian honesty should prompt her to delegate her authority generously to others and to allow them to use this shared power with responsible freedom. She will understand that general and broad permissions given to sisters not only are lawful aspects of religious obedience, but necessary to facilitate intelligently the work of sisters in a modern apostolate. Humble sincerity will make her objective in interpreting the rule liberally according to the needs of sisters, and in granting the exceptions necessary to enlightened adaptation in any particular circumstance.

Private and arbitrary interpretation of rules and customs by superiors without consideration for the underlying spirit of the Community can be an unfair imposition of personal opinion on sisters, and normally makes for dissatisfaction among sisters and inefficiency in apostolic work. A mature religious superior always is alert and sensitive in distinguishing between the end—the fullness of Christian love—and the means of attaining it.

Much has been said about the practice of charity among sisters and superiors in religious life. But several other fundamental understandings, important to the attitudes of all sisters to conventual superiorship, should be emphasized here. Once a sister has been appointed a superior, she need not always be a superior. Sisters should learn to move comfortably and securely from one role to another, without feeling they have been cheated or demoted if they are not re-appointed to a second or a third term of superiorship. Reasonably frequent replacements of administrators in religious life are healthy and good for the progress of the community, the satisfaction of the sisters, and the mental health of superiors. All sisters should be so completely developed as Christians that higher superiors will have no difficulty finding mature people to appoint as superiors.

Too often, the superiorship is regarded by sisters as a reward for fidelity, a sign of prestige, or as a token of victory, rather than as a position of service to others. The idea of "grace of office" has been abused by sisters and misinterpreted to mean many things which it is not. Actually, it means that when a sister is appointed as a superior she will receive the graces from God which are necessary for her to fulfill her duties effectively. In the same way, the fourth grade teacher, the convent housekeeper, or the private secretary to the Provincial Superior all get the graces they need to accomplish their tasks. It does not, in any way, indicate that the superior is better than the other sisters, that she is always right in making decisions or in organizing projects, that she has dogmatic excellence of any kind, that she has infused virtue or automatic holiness, that she is omniscient, or that she has any right to infringe on the personal privacy of sisters.

A superior is a human woman who, as the superior of a community of sisters, should be the mature mother of mature daughters. To be a mature mother to mature daughters is not an easy task for a religious superior. It is quite different from mothering children and it is well that some consideration be given to the qualities of a religious superior who will be able maturely to communicate Christian love to her sisters.

Besides the mature qualities which should be possessed by all sisters, it is particularly important that a superior be a prudent, balanced woman with a good sense of values. She must love people and know that in her love, interest, and time, they always take precedence over things. This means, among other things, that the superior will be habitually approachable. A superior cannot afford to be tempermental; she must be predictable so sisters can know what to expect from her. She must be objective, so she can rise above her personal feelings in any situation, seeing reality as it is and not as it affects her. Because she is honest and sincere, she knows that as a superior she is not on a psychological pedestal. Her primary role is not that of model. The inspiration she gives by her good example will be an incidental benefit of her motherliness to sisters. She deals with sisters in genuine love, warmth, enthusiasm, humor, and kindness. A superior must be flexible; she must know when to make exceptions in community living. She realizes that she is the custodian of the spirit of the rule and that the letter of the rule must be adjusted to the spirit which motivates it. And, in all events, exceptions must be granted in consideration of individual problems.

A superior takes the sisters under her direction and into her heart and loves them. She does not, however, take them on her conscience and make herself liable for their shortcomings or their mistakes. She only has to provide circumstances or arrange details so that sisters can do what is expected of them as religious women. A superior must decide what is important and not get so tangled in details that she cannot sift the relevant from the irrelevant or the important from the unimportant in dealing with sisters. She must be truly open-minded; that is, broadminded with a conscience. In working with sisters a superior always places more emphasis on coordination than on conformity. Rigidity and regimentation are never the answer in working with human beings.

A superior must be reasonably calm and level-headed. She has to have the strength to make decisions and the courage to implement them, but she can never afford to be shocked. She must always understand that any problem that is peculiar to human beings is also possible to sisters. She must endeavor to have the foresight, the tact, the good judgment, and the patience to deal with them maturely. A superior should not always look for trouble—there is enough of it without making difficulties where there are none. She should expect problems since they are human, but not create them. She can never solve all problems, but must aim to understand them and to make them less painful or annoying for the persons concerned.

A mature superior knows better than to take anything in community life as a personal affront. Most of the time even things which seem personally hurting really are not meant in that way. It is balancing to accept them as objectively as possible. There is time enough for the superior to be hurt when someone tells her that they intended a personal slight or offense. Even in such instances, the wise superior who understands human nature knows that patient understanding is the only intelligent antidote against such an admission. Undoubtedly, many such admissions are made with haste in the heat of emotion, and sincerely regretted soon after, or are made by a person who needs assistance in living more rationally.

A superior must consider the problems of the sisters under her direction as the sisters see them. In other words, she must attempt to establish their point of view. The importance of any human problem is not always gauged intrinsically, but by its effect on the person who is harrassed by it. If a superior is to help a sister in her difficulties, she must have the ability to listen with warmth and understanding. She must be genuinely concerned. She gives the sister credit for sincerity, and accepts her views and reactions, even though she may not be able to agree with them. Many times a sister just needs someone to listen to her story. Other times, she may need someone to help her get a proper perspective so she can make a rational decision. In still other situations, she may need someone to honestly and firmly exert the discipline that she would like to exert on herself.

A superior should be totally trustworthy in respecting a sister's confidences. A sister must feel secure with her mother! She must always be able to count on her understanding and sincerity. The reliable superior never shuns her responsibility to help sisters by immediately directing them to "offer it up," or to "to to the chapel and tell God about it." At best, these recommendations are pietistic at this point. A sister who is emotionally upset needs the human release and relief which will ordinarily follow communication with someone who understands. Then the sister will be open to suggestions of genuine spiritual depth.

Religious superiors should be fair to sisters, not by treating them all alike, but by giving them all equal acceptance and appreciation as individual persons. No sister should feel "left out" of the love of her superior. It is tragic that sometimes a sister's acceptance in a community depends on whether or not the superior likes her. If a superior is mature, she will be just in appraising each sister as a person. If she is not, she may tend to evaluate sisters on an arbitrary or whimsical basis. The opinion of a superior is a very significant matter to each sister, whether she is willing to admit it or not, especially since it is possible that for some sisters personal security in the community may depend on it.

Sisters look to their superiors for the understanding, loyalty, trust, and honesty they should be able to expect from a mature mother. The task of being a mature mother to mature daughters is a classic challenge of Christian love for religious superiors who take their obligations seriously. Very special vision and prudence should be used in selecting sisters for this tremendous service of Christian love.

Conclusion

The mature sister knows it is a tremendous experience to be human **and** realizes that if she is to be apostolically effective at all, she must aim to become as magnificently human as is possible. She approaches life and relates to people with a holy verve and vitality which expresses itself with dignified propriety according to her temperament. Out of this comes the joy, peace, warmth, and approachableness which are so essential in her dealings with people. The sister who is enthusiastic is eager and willing to serve others, and offers her services, not condescendingly, but with Christ-like graciousness. She expresses the love that is her motivating force in such warmth and congeniality, typically her own, that all those she contacts are ultimately attracted by it—to Christ. It becomes the bond between people and the Heart of God, with the sister as the mediator.

The sister who is enthusiastic never works "just to be doing a job" or "just because it is part of the daily schedule." She serves others because she loves them for their own sakes, and, as a result, the entire apostolate is more vibrant because she is there. Love is the secret and source of her genuine influence. When love of Christ, which is the heart of the religious woman's life, is missing, the essence of apostolic activity is gone, and work becomes impersonal, cold, and unproductive—in spite of high-powered efficiency. People are looking for the real happiness which comes from genuine service. They look to the sister in the modern world to show them the way to love.

Joy is the hallmark of the Christian commitment of love— and people expect to find it in a special way in the sister who has pledged herself to it. And if it doesn't consistently show through the happiness in her face, the optimism in her attitudes, the enthusiasm in her actions, and the song in her heart, they will never believe her when she says the religious life is a happy state!

Christian life with God and His business of love as its purpose is stimulating. It is not adolescent adulation or superficial hilarity. Rather, it is the thrill of wonder at the constant unfolding of the living reality of God in all people and things. When a sister lacks this holy spirit of adventure, when she loses the thrill of Christian love and no longer sees God as central in the prosaic circumstances of her religious vocation, then life becomes dull for her.

She is apathetic—the victim of boredom and selfishness. A religious woman whose life has become routinely self-centered is a tragedy. She is only a shell—a symbol of barren emptiness who shatters the hopes of those who look to her for courage and inspiration. She is cold, discontented, unproductive, fearful, and unpredictable. She is dead as an instrument of Christian love. She not only fails to contribute, but definitely hinders the work of the apostolate.

On the other hand, a sister who lives her vocation of love completely is a sensitive, vigorous, happy agent of love in the Christian family. She is a woman of great, generous vision, capable of enlarged thinking and dynamic loving, who makes a constructive impact on the world in which she lives. Through her is communicated the message of Christian love—the megatonic power which motivates all apostolic action. This is the sister, who, because of a sense of responsibility and a sympathetic relevance to the immediate world, communicates to all the meaning of love as it is lived by Christians. This is a challenge which, when enthusiastically accepted by a sister, sparks the heroism of young and old to live the Christian identification—LOVE—which Christ has prescribed for His followers. Christ! Heaven! The perfection and completion of Christian love will be her eternal compensation!